# The Dynamics of
# EFFECTIVE NEGOTIATION
### Second Edition

**Gulf Publishing Company**
Houston, London, Paris, Zurich, Tokyo

# The Dynamics of EFFECTIVE NEGOTIATION

## Second Edition

*A win/win approach to getting what you want*

• • • • • • • • • • • • • • • • • • • • • • • • • • • •

## Donald B. Sparks

*to Danna Sue,*
*who combines charm*
*with purpose*

# The Dynamics of Effective Negotiation
## Second Edition

Gulf Publishing Company
Book Division
P.O. Box 2608
Houston, Texas 77252-2608

**Library of Congress Cataloging-in-Publication Data**

Sparks, Donald B.
    The dynamics of effective negotiation/Donald B. Sparks.—2nd ed.
        p.   cm.
    Includes bibliographical references and index.
    **ISBN 0-88415-102-6**
    1. Negotiation in business.  I. Title.
    HD58.6.S63  1993
    658.4—dc20                                          93-23839
                                                           CIP

10   9   8   7   6   5   4   3   2   1

# Contents

# Foreword

Today, the negotiation process has captured public interest. Corporate and public executives see it as a pragmatic way to attain organizational goals. Long before this process became so popular, Don Sparks was helping people develop negotiating skills, using illustrations of appropriate negotiating techniques that produce success. Improperly used, these techniques can result in failure; therefore the importance of understanding Don Sparks' general methods and approach when tackling specific negotiating situations.

Applying Sparks' methods to negotiating problems can result in agreements that need not be constantly monitored and reworked, thereby saving much valuable time. The general approach of this book centers on long-range relationships, with a balanced emphasis on present, competitively sought objectives. A grasp of this book's teachings will help any negotiator achieve maximum effectiveness and greater professionalism.

Jerry P. Clousson, J.D., L.L.M.
Director, Department of Negotiations
American Medical Association

[J. P. Clousson, now practices law in Chicago specializing in health maintenance organizations and professional medical groups]

# Preface

Negotiation is an attempt to get agreement on an issue, problem, or question over which two or more parties disagree. The aim of this book is to improve how negotiations are done by using a systematic approach.

A systematic approach goes a long way toward reaching three goals. First, it helps settle more issues successfully. A win-win does this when possible. Second, it builds trust, respect, and commitment between parties that have on-going negotiations. This means fostering a long-term relationship valued by both parties. Third, it minimizes the time spent in negotiations by doing them well. This requires producing genuinely sound resolutions that can be carried out.

*The Dynamics of Effective Negotiation* is unlike other books about negotiations. It shows the merits of conducting negotiations pragmatically versus considering them an art form. It accentuates the areas that experience shows are critical to successful negotiations. Negotiators must prepare for negotiations using a step-by-step method. This goes beyond experience and knowledge. Negotiators also must adopt an issue orientation. Negotiating "style" is important, but it is secondary to issues.

The bulk of current literature on negotiations emphasizes me-versus-you strategies, out-and-out use of gimmicks, and techniques unsubstantiated by research. This emphasis is misplaced. It leads to relying on win-lose actions. It also denies scientific findings of intergroup psychological research. These findings describe:

- methods for merging the actions of individuals or groups into productive channels; and
- techniques for reducing unproductive conflicts.

This book's techniques will help negotiators at all levels of experience. The methods provided resolve issues fairly, even when other parties challenge with methods geared to one-way resolution. The emphasis is on resolving issues based on the merits of both parties' positions. The techniques for this are explained. Examples illustrate how the techniques work. Guidelines for when and where to use them are provided.

All the gimmicks known, including intimidation, shatter like glass when thrown against the rock of win-win negotiations. Agreements forged through win-win negotiations have a high probability of enactment. This is because issue resolution in win-win negotiations is based on merit - on what should be. This is its major strength. Experience shows that most people will stick to equitable agreements. Also, win-win negotiations avoid residual hostilities that damage post-agreement follow-through.

The weakness in non-win-win negotiating methods is that issues are often not resolved. The use of intimidation, power, or time pressure forces agreement. These methods leave the question of issue merit unsettled. Unresolved merit questions are latent sources of problems. These arise at the most inconvenient times.

The approaches described are designed for industrial use. Modified, they can be applied to personal negotiations. The original book concentrated on negotiations in the industrialized western countries. This revision includes data useful for international negotiations.

To become proficient with the win-win approach, negotiators must understand and accept four things. These are the main parts of this book.
1. The characteristics of negotiations (Chapters 1-4).
2. The need for disciplined, diligent preparation (Chapters 5-6).
3. The use of common-sense methods for conducting negotiations (Chapter 7-11).
4. The skills required to work effectively with style-oriented opponents (Chapters 12-14).

The terms "negotiator[s]" and "opponent[s]" throughout this book describe the two parties in a negotiation. "Negotiator[s]" denotes skilled individuals using a win-win approach. "Opponent[s]" signify people opposing negotiators. They have many styles and approaches to negotiating. Opponents may be as skilled as negotiators. There is no implication they should be underrated. The goal is learning to work successfully with others who do not share the win-win approach to negotiating.

Donald B. Sparks
Houston, Texas

# Acknowledgments

My appreciation goes to Robert Aldag, III, Contracting Department, Arabian American Oil Company (now President of the Marine Preservation Association); James Jeffries, Coca-Cola Foods Division, Coca-Cola Company; E. J. Townsend, Jr., General Systems Division, International Business Machines Corporation; Monty Stone, Vice President of Allright Corporation; Steven Hirsch, Vice President -Operations, Voluntary Hospitals of Iowa, and Mrs. Danna W. Sparks for their able assistance in preparation and editing of the book's first and second editions. A note of thanks goes to the more than 41,000 participants in my Negotiating Skills Improvement seminars conducted since 1975. These seminars provided the opportunity for synthesizing material into this revised edition. Equally important has been the refinement of my own ideas about negotiating from consulting work with clients.

# PART I

# THE NEGOTIATION PROCESS

## The beginning.

The history of negotiating can be traced to 1000 B.C. Up to that time, societies lived in self-contained units. The Greek City-States of Athens and Sparta are examples. Then some Greeks went west to Ionia on the Aegean coast. They had a tough time making it since mountains blocked inland growth. These Greeks turned to the sea to make a living. They had to trade with mainlanders who were Persian and Arab. The trade required negotiating. That is where it all started.

# CHAPTER 1

# *CHARACTERISTICS OF THE NEGOTIATING SITUATION*

*The North Wind and the Sun*

*The North Wind and the Sun disputed as to which was the most powerful, and they agreed that he should be declared the victor who could first strip a wayfaring man of his clothes. The North Wind first tried his power and blew with all his might, but the keener his blasts, the closer the traveler wrapped his cloak around him, until at last, resigning all hope of victory, the Wind called upon the Sun to see what he could do. The Sun suddenly shone out with all his warmth. The traveler no sooner felt his genial rays than he took off one garment after another, and, at last, fairly overcome with heat, undressed and bathed in a stream that lay in his path.*

Persuasion is better than force.
Aesop's Fables

## THE FIVE NEGOTIATING CHARACTERISTICS

Negotiating situations have five characteristics.

1. Exchange, giving and taking between two parties.
2. Restraints and drives, resulting in friction between the parties.
3. An important issue that both parties seek to resolve.
4. Uncertainty.

5. Real or perceived conflict between the parties' positions.

## Exchange

Negotiations involve an exchange of giving and taking between negotiators and opponents. Through this exchange, they attempt to reach an agreeable or acceptable conclusion in settling an issue. Negotiators expect opponents to move from their original positions toward the negotiators', and vice versa. Concessions are part of this movement. Readjusting goals is also part. Differences in concern about the various issues is a third part. For example, one party may have only one issue of prime importance while the other party has three. The amount of movement decides, in the end, which party got more of its aims.

The exchange presents a special problem for numerically oriented people. They prefer many wins, though each may be small in importance. These people are apt to pass by a major issue in exchange for several minor issues. Goal congruity in planning for negotiations helps prevent negotiators from slipping into a numerical orientation. Goal congruity keeps the focus on the goal wanted and progress toward it.

Failure to stick to a quid pro quo philosophy reduces chances of negotiators being successful. Quid pro quo means "something for something." Opponents who get concessions without giving any expect that other concessions are available without cost. Any different behavior, such as negotiators expecting return concessions, surprises opponents. There should be no free lunches.

The win-win approach highlights the issue being negotiated. Issues might be quantitative. Examples are the amount of service to be given, or number of items involved, or price or cost. Or issues might be qualitative, such as a company's image or industry practice. Personalities are definitely not the concern in win-win negotiations. They are left out of the deliberation. Chapter 6 includes discussion of methods for controlling reaction to opponents' personalities.

## Example

A negotiator has two negotiations scheduled. The first is settling a $1,000,000 claim against their company by a contractor. This is an important issue because of the:

- amount involved;
- future relations with contractors; and
- potential creation of a practice or position affecting such claims.

To negotiate the claim properly, a negotiator invests the time and energy to deal with its importance. The negotiator negotiates at a level commensurate to the issue's importance.

The second negotiation is with a maintenance contractor. Low-bid policy dictated the contractor selection. The negotiation will concentrate on settling the contractor schedules. It also may examine how payments are made - lump sum, progress, or a combination of the two.

This second negotiation is less important than the first on two counts. It has lower economic value and policy limits the amount of influence on the outcome. The negotiator spends less time on the second issue.

---

**Guideline:** The objective of skilled negotiators is to negotiate at the level of the issues. Level means the importance of the issues. Major issues get more time and effort. Every issue is not treated the same.

---

## Friction

The exchange in negotiations is uncomfortable, even stressful. The Latin meaning of the word negotiate is "neg" for not and "otium" for ease. Until the negotiation reaches agreement, a person is not at ease. The friction is produced by two forces that operate in opposite directions within each party. The forces are restraints and drives.

Restraints operate to retard progress. They are questions: What am I going to gain or lose for my side? Is the other party trustworthy? What effect might this agreement have on our competition? Drives operate to push progress toward resolution. They are needs. Examples are: wanting to cooperate with others; wanting to influence others; hoping for a successful conclusion.

The intensity of friction caused by restraints and drives converts into stress felt by each party. A person's emotional maturity and self-discipline decide how stress is handled.

Chapter 6 discusses ways to increase self-discipline.

## Importance

Negotiations are reserved for situations requiring serious effort - those for which other methods of conclusion are less suitable. This raises the question of how negotiators should allot time to do the tasks needed. There is a practical way to increase the time available for negotiating. And it does not take time from other, equally important work. Negotiators simply clear off items from their negotiating workload that can be dealt with in other ways. The procedure for this clear off is straightforward.

1. List all issues negotiated.
2. Analyze each issue based on the factors considered important.
3. Make a disposition for each issue: keep, reassign, or relegate it to a procedure.

Figure 1-1 presents a layout for compiling the list, evaluating the relative worth of each issue, and making the disposition. It might require one day or several to gather sufficient information. The issues represent the extent and variety with which a negotiator deals. After making the disposition, the amount of negotiating time may be the same. But the focus is redirected to issues with the potential to produce the best payout for the effort made. Four points are observed in making the disposition.

1. Frequently recurring issues are good targets for control through procedure.
2. Issues having multiple uses or potential for increased economic benefit to the organization need greater attention.
3. Static issues still needing negotiation are delegated to others.
4. Some issues can be eliminated. They are not negotiable, not tied to the organization's objectives, or not important. These are usually around because of a negotiator's personal preference.

Time allocation is part of planning for negotiations. There are two options for gaining more negotiating time. Use time more efficiently. Or expand it by reducing other work time or adding more hours.

---

**Guideline:** Disciplined negotiators review the allocation of their negotiating efforts regularly.

---

## Uncertainty

Negotiations are inherently uncertain. They require a situational approach. Negotiation is too complex a process to base strategy mostly on past, proven experiences. Personal experiences shape ideas about negotiations. They lead to telltale habits and predictable patterns. These become liabilities for nego-

| Item | $ Value | Frequency | | | Hrs | $ Impor- tance | Disposition |
|---|---|---|---|---|---|---|---|
| | | D | W | M | | | |
| Expedite spare parts contracts | 200 | | 1 | | 2 | 50 | Delegate |
| Order office materials | 90 | 2 | | | 1 | | Make a procedure |
| Review and re-negotiate claims on delay | 3000 | | | 1 | 15 | 2000 | Keep |
| Special price concessions on all large orders | 1000 | | 1 | | ? | 300 | Keep |
| Check on lead-time revision possibilities | 300 | 1 | | | 8 | 50 | Delegate |

**Figure 1-1.** Finding where negotiating time is spent. (Source: Sparks Consultants.)

tiators. They are opportunities for undeserved gain for opponents. Negotiators must be flexible. Adopting an issue orientation best achieves it. This does not mean changing personality. It means locking onto the issue, selecting a strategy that is comfortable to use, and adopting tactics fitting a negotiator's skills.

Chapter 5 discusses methods that aid in gaining and retaining an issue orientation.

## Conflict

Conflict exists between the positions of the parties in negotiations. While its intensity varies, conflict is an important ingredient in negotiations. Without it, there is little motivation for working hard to find a good solution. Negotiators able to distinguish between common disagreement and conflict appreciate conflict's role.

Disagreement is any difference between two parties. However, disagreement does not result in a collision between those two parties, due to a collision between their goals.

There are three types of conflict: resource, pathway, and value. These types always occur in combination. Negotiators must recognize them and identify which dominates the issue. Two types of conflict are easier to deal with; they lend themselves to quantitative assessment or, at least, to definitions.

In resource conflict, mutually exclusive goals are the aim of each party because of limits on time, money, space, etc. If one party gets its goal, the other cannot. Resources are not available for satisfying both goals.

In resource conflict using a win-win approach, each party strives to gain a victory over the other. The victory results from issue resolution largely based on the merits of the two parties' positions. This contrasts with trying to defeat or suppress the other party, as in win-lose. A win-win victory by one party does not stigmatize the other party. The victory may involve only one issue out of several. A win-win settlement is not equally favorable to both parties. However, both parties can support the settlement since the conflict is reduced without personal abuse or intimidation.

In pathway conflict, the dispute centers on how something should be done. Agreement on the goal is not a question.

## Example

The chief executive of a manufacturing company announces a drive to increase profit. Part of the drive is reducing expenses. The marketing people suggest cutting General and Administrative expenses. The manufacturing people suggest increasing the length of product runs to minimize set-up costs. Both responses are correct as far as their proponents' views. Where options of approximate equal value exist, the option selected should be the result of negotiation.

In pathway conflict, each party supports achievement of an accepted goal based on concern for its own position. In reducing pathway conflict, a loss of confidence by one party in the other must be avoided. Again, the best opportunity for an acceptable settlement is a win-win attitude focusing on the issue. One that will be supported later.

The third type of conflict is the toughest with which to deal. Negotiators need to recognize this kind of conflict quickly. It must be handled differently than the other two kinds. Otherwise there is the risk of becoming involved in drawn-out negotiations, often over non-essential or hard-to-define issues. Value conflict is emotionally linked to a belief. The belief arouses responses that ignore facts. People do not easily change these types of intense feelings. Negotiators, no matter how skillful, may not be able to influence them.

## Examples

To understand value differences, look at values attributed to life forms. Imagine killing in order a lettuce, fly, frog, cat and chimpanzee. The kill gets tougher as the victim's level on the life form scale rises.

A contractor's proposal for an oversea's construction job stipulates first-class travel and luxury housing for its employees. The contractor says that its policy calls for these two actions. The customer responds that its policy is to furnish tourist travel and economy housing. Travel and housing do not fit directly with work quality or schedule in the customer's view. But the issue is an important one in value conflict. Will contractor personnel feel better enough about first-class travel and luxury housing to do a better job? Will those things motivate them to complete the work ahead of schedule? What is the benefit to the customer? How is that benefit measured? Perhaps the contractor should pay the extra amount if it matters so much. Is this really the customer's problem? This conflict has more to do with feelings than fact.

When confronted with an issue dominated by value conflict, negotiators have several options. There is a specific order in which these options should be tried.

1. Let opponents vent their feelings about the issue. Do not challenge those feelings.
2. Proceed without acknowledgment. This ignores the opponents' basic direction. Sometimes just venting is enough to get them over the hurdle. Break away for a recess to give opponents time to cool down. They can conveniently resume on a rational note.
3. Seek to identify issues of approximate equal value and attraction to opponents. Those issues might be substituted for the ones causing value conflicts. This is difficult. It involves a complex psychological transfer. If a substitute issue is found, it can be given to the opponent at the right time. Doing this increases chances to resolve original issues realistically.
4. Never give in to a value-based position. That leads to larger value-based demands. Aborting the negotiation is better than falling down an endless tube of irrational, unrealistic demands chain-linked by emotion.

Two additional points regarding conflict are worth remembering because they are a double jeopardy. The longer a conflict exists, the more likely its importance escalates. Figure 1-2 shows this change. Furthermore, unresolved conflicts distort the importance of future conflicts. They are intensified.

---

**Guideline:** It is best to try to resolve all the issues or to dispose of them by mutual accord. Any that are unresolved will pop up at the worst possible time.

---

## Hidden Conflicts

Negotiators need to be aware of two hidden sources of conflicts. These may be unrelated to the issues being negotiated. They affect relationships between parties anyway. The first source of hidden conflict is economic. It comes from one party having an unconsumed economic desire. For example, a person wants a luxury automobile but does not earn enough to get it. That person may blame their money shortage on the other party. The equation for this is:

$$\text{ECONOMIC SUCCESS} = \frac{\text{CONSUMPTION}}{\text{DESIRE}}$$

People judge their economic success by the amount of desire consumed.

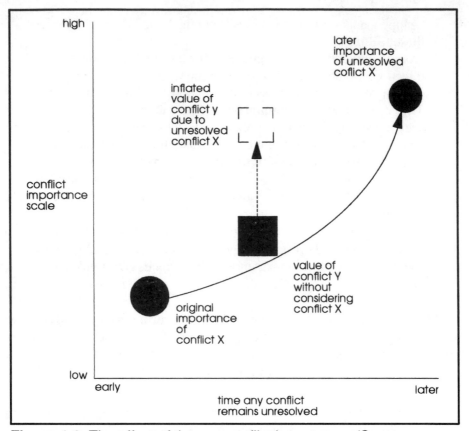

**Figure 1-2.** The effect of time on conflict importance. (Source: Games People Play, E. Berne.)

The second hidden source of conflict comes from one party having an unreached aspiration. For example, a person wants a better title than their job warrants. That person may blame their lack of wanted title on the other party. The equation for this is:

$$\text{PERSONAL SUCCESS} = \frac{\text{ACHIEVEMENT}}{\text{ASPIRATION}}$$

People judge their personal success by the amount of aspiration achieved.

In hidden conflicts, the party blamed knows that something is complicating the relationship. But not what it is. Nor will they find out. Hidden conflicts often exist between superiors and  subordinates in organizations. Also between peers.

The next chapter examines the possible outcomes from negotiations.

# CHAPTER 2

# *NEGOTIATING OUTCOMES*

### The Two Frogs

*Two Frogs dwelt in the same pool. When the pool dried up under the summer's heat, they left it and set out together for another home. As they went along they chanced to pass a deep well, amply supplied with water, and when they saw it, one of the Frogs said to the other, "Let us descend and make our abode in this well; it will furnish us with shelter and food." The other replied with greater caution, "But suppose the water should fail us. How can we get out again from so great a depth?"*

Do nothing without regard to the consequences.
Aesop's Fables

Negotiations' outcomes are viewed as positive or negative. The view is based more on how the outcome is obtained, the methods used, and less on its quality or correctness. There are three positive outcomes.

1. Solution.
2. Compromise.
3. Correction.

There are three negative outcomes.

1. Imposition.
2. Surrender.
3. Stalemate.

## Positive Outcomes

Solution, compromise, and correction produce satisfactory agreements. They are, therefore, positive. Both parties see these agreements as beneficial and fair.

## Solutions

Solutions are rare. They come about when negotiators and opponents get all they want. In such cases, the negotiation takes place because of requirements or false impressions for its need. Real conflict did not exist. The requirements might be procedural, regulatory, etc.

## Example

A company requires a contract for all expenditures greater than $ 10,000. The company wants a technological device from a sole source. Contract negotiation centers on terms and conditions. The goal sought by the supplier is the price. The customer is willing to pay, since the device is not available elsewhere. Both parties encounter little difficulty getting their major goals.

The solution example could become an adjustment example. The parties might encounter minor differences and have to work through them before resolution. Agreements negotiated by solution or adjustment usually are successful.

## Compromise

In compromise, negotiators and opponents give in on some parts of their major and, probably, minor goals. They do so to get closure on other parts. Compromise occurs more than solution or adjustment. When one party is giving during compromise, it tries to minimize its loss. Each party's negotiating skills greatly influence the content of compromise outcomes. Compromise results in negotiators and opponents sharing in the winning. The sharing is seldom equal.

Agreements negotiated by compromise have a great chance of success. They require more follow up than do agreements resulting from solution or adjustment.

## Correction

Correction occurs when one party uses wrong data to support its position.

This is embarrassing when the other party proves the use of faulty data, insupportable conclusions, etc.  Correction is usually caused by sloppy preparation. Sometimes it is from a lapse in judgment.

Corrections to one party usually mean a clear win by the other party.  It is a positive outcome because it is done to oneself. Negotiators enduring a correction should take three actions.

1. Admit the error.  Why waste everyone's time trying to argue away what is obvious?  Error admission helps build trust with opponents. Something is salvaged.
2. Limit the correction to the issue.  Do not let it be expanded to other issues.  A negotiator's information can be invalid about a specific issue. It does not follow that their other information is also wrong.
3. Take a recess.  This avoids any psychological let down carrying over to weaken negotiator resolve on the next issue.  Also, it takes the edge off the unearned advantage handed an opponent.  However, negotiators should remember that what happens just before a recess influences thinking during the recess.  The recess gives time to learn whether an error occurred or mitigating factors exist.

Chapter 5 presents methods that minimize the chance negotiators will experience a correction.

## Negative Outcomes

The next three outcomes do not resolve the issue.  But they may result in an agreement.  In brief, the conflict remains.  The settlement is very likely to be temporary.  Sometimes a temporary settlement is better than alternatives.

### Imposition

Imposition happens because one party is in a position of almost total power. It can push its way over the other party no matter the merit of either side's position.  Using intimidating tactics is a form of imposition.

### Example

An opponent may threaten legal action over a disputed issue if their demands for a settlement are not met.  The negotiator feels the demands are excessive.  However, the negotiator may decide it is more costly to litigate than to settle.  If the opponent's demands are met in this way, is the issue really settled?  Probably not.

Experience shows that intimidated parties continually seek to undo imposed
agreements.  They also try to position themselves to return the favor, so to
speak.  Imposing goals through power is a shortsighted way to negotiate.
Another form of imposition is the use of time.  One party tries to wear out the
other party, to win through attrition.  The goal is to weaken others by creating
a sense of futility of ever getting their views appreciated.  Another form of
time imposition is where one party urgently needs what the imposing party
can provide.  Again, the issue is not resolved based on merit.  It is, therefore,
still open.  Eventually, the time pressure runs out.  Then, the party that yielded
to it becomes resolute in its own demands.  Imposition always causes a
win-lose outcome, real or perceived.  There is dissatisfaction about the agreement.  And there is damage to future relations between the parties.

One response to imposition is asking the party doing the imposing this
question.  "Is it in your interest to leave us hostile by forcing your position
through power?  Is it not better to stick to the merits of our differing views and
let that direct the agreement?"

## Surrender

Surrender happens when one party is persuaded that it will suffer more by
getting what it wants than by giving in.  Success looks more costly than gain.
An example is a supplier who pushes through a stiff immediate price increase
over customer objections.  The customer seeks other supply sources.  It sees
the increase as unjustified.  Surrenders sometimes occur because of pressure
from higher authority within an organization.

## Example

A foreign government selected a U.S. contractor to build a large
chemical processing plant.  It was a turnkey job.  The contract
negotiation was important to both parties.  The customer set the
negotiating period for November.  The customer intentionally
slowed negotiating progress.  Executives of the parent of the contractor, a publicly listed company, pressured the contractor to make
concessions.  The parent wanted to announce the backlog in its
fourth quarter financial statement.  That would help its performance picture within the investment community.  Research by the
foreign government into U.S. business practice paid off.

Generally, surrender results in unwarranted settlements.  Like imposition, surrender leaves the question of issue merit undealt with and the issue unresolved. Surrender, unlike imposition, may avoid harming future relations. But circumstances often arise during agreement enactment that resurrect the issue.

What can be learned from reviewing the experiences following imposition and surrender? Just this. If the issue is not settled, it does not often go away.

## Stalemate

Stalemate occurs three ways. First, neither party wants to continue toward a settlement. Both adopt fixed, entrenched positions. Or neither party sees any benefit from creating a change that allows progress toward settlement. Second, stalemate can result from each party believing it can afford to wait out the other. Third, the stalemate is a tactic to force the negotiation to a higher authority level. Negotiators encountering a stalemate should explore options before accepting a total breakdown. The following options are in order of how easy they are to use.

1. Restate the issue in question. This ensures that everyone is thinking of the same thing in the same way. It finds if the stalemate is real. If there is misunderstanding, restatement clears it up. Progress resumes.
2. Take a recess. Then start fresh. Perhaps everyone is overtired. Recess length depends on the circumstances. Did one party travel a long distance? Are there separate rooms where each party can caucus or relax?
3. Introduce new information. Try to change the scope or shape of the issue causing the hangup. Perhaps its importance can be changed by combining it with an issue to be introduced later.
4. Set-aside the issue temporarily. Write it down so that both parties agree on the description. When resuming the issue, there will be no question about its content, scope, etc. Put the written material in plain view. Agree either party can reintroduce the issue when either wants. Go to another issue. The set-aside is a potent method for moving issues to more favorable slots on an agenda. It changes the order of issue discussion. Set-asides work especially well in three circumstances. The first is when an issue is out of sequence to others. This may be due to poor planning, assumption errors, etc. The second is when feelings of one or both parties become intense enough to override legitimate discussion. This may be due to loss of selfcontrol. The third is when not enough trust has developed to discuss a sensitive issue. Set-asides have other potential outcomes. One is that on returning to the issue, both parties may hold to their original positions. They are no better off than before. They are also no worse off.

A stalemate may recur. The other potential outcome is that set-aside may evolve into withdrawal of the issue. The initiative of the parties may be dampened. Set-asides are underutilized.

5. Change one or both people representing the parties. This should always be done by joint agreement. Substituting people removes carrying forward unfavorable reactions between the original parties. These reactions may not be anyone's fault. They can result from poor personal chemistry. The change also removes the onerous effect of statements by the original people. The argument against changing people in the negotiation has two premises. The first is that the suggestion for the change is perceived as a sign of weakness by opponents. That does not necessarily follow. But if it was an opponent's conclusion, it would be temporary. When new negotiators turn out not to be weak, opponents abandon that premise. The second premise is that the change might cause a loss of position. Nuances that make intent clear are not easily communicated to the new people. This risk must be assessed when judging whether changing the parties makes sense.

6. Forego negotiation and move to mediation or arbitration. Introducing a third party changes the process. The influence of the original two parties is irrevocably reduced. Three parties are a different type of exchange than negotiations. If avoiding a total breakdown is important and nothing else does it, a third party is warranted. This should be a last step. Mediators are only deemed successful when both sides are equally unhappy. Arbitrators remove the parties from the decision process. They make binding decisions based on representations by the parties.

In general, successful outcomes require effort, patience, and fairness. These must be balanced by negotiator competitiveness and stubborn commitment.

The next chapter examines the use of negotiating teams.

# CHAPTER 3

# *USE OF TEAMS*

*The Father and His Sons*

*A Father had a family of sons who were perpetually quarreling among themselves. When he failed to heal their disputes by his exhortations, he determined to give them a practical illustration of the evils of disunion; and for this purpose he one day told them to bring him a bundle of sticks. When they had done so, he placed the bundle into the hands of each of them in succession and ordered them to break it in pieces. They tried with all their strength, and were not able to do it. He next opened the bundle, took the sticks separately, one by one, and again put them into his sons' hands, upon which they broke them easily. He then addressed them in these words: "My sons, if you are of one mind, and unite to assist each other, you will be as this bundle, uninjured by all the attempts of your enemies; but if you are divided among yourselves, you will be broken as easily as these sticks."*

Aesop's Fables

## The Use of Teams

The use of teams to negotiate is increasing. There are good reasons. First, negotiations are more complex, partly due to growing litigiousness in the private sector. This adds to the difficulty of doing business. Second, as more knowledge is available about every field, individuals are more specialized. It is increasingly tough for one person to know enough to conduct any but simple negotiations. Third, teams provide witnesses to what is said. Teams reduce second guessing from others not present at the negotiations. There are more people who know how, what, and why agreements were reached.

## Team Value

One-half the value of teams is their wider view when examining issues. Each person on the team is the sum of their experience, intelligence, physical drive, biases, etc. These factors are a person's capacity base. By adding people, a partial overlap in these bases occurs. However, the nonoverlapping areas extend the capacity base of the team. Figure 3-1 shows this phenomenon.

The other half of team value is that negotiation involves three distinct roles. These are the talker, writer, and listener. It is difficult for one person to do all three well. Two people can do them well. Three are ideal.

Talkers give positions on issues. Talkers do the negotiating. One talker is all that is needed. Talkers must think quickly.

Talkers simultaneously must arrange items by priority and relate these to their total goals. Talker's must use clear terms, build good examples, be sensitive to timing, and understanding of others. Common sense and judgment are absolutes for effectiveness as a talker. The style of presentation may range from "country" to "smooth." Style is of secondary importance. Talkers have the most active of the three roles. It consumes the most energy. Stamina is an important asset for anyone filling this role. Talkers should not reach agreement on issues without checking with their team members first.

Writers must be good judges of when their side makes a concession or gets one. Writers instinctively know what to keep in notes. Writers must record things while listening to following discussion. They must evaluate agreements clearly, write concisely, have excellent memory. A human recorder is much better than a machine. Not all of the conversation that takes place needs to be kept. A review of the complete recordings of a sample of ten negotiations shows this. Some were as brief as half a day, and one required a week. The critical data, based on the total number of minutes, ranged from 6% to 23%. However, a caution is necessary about recording in any form. Later, a legal dispute about the negotiations might happen. Any record could be called for during what the lawyers call "discovery". Retaining negotiation meeting records must be assessed against the risk of their being used in litigation. On balance, it is generally best to have well kept and accurate notes. This should not be a problem in legitimate negotiations.

## Example

A Federal Trade Commission [FTC] price discrimination hearing dealt with price breaks a manufacturer gave to large distributors. An executive of the manufacturer kept notes during negotiations with these distributors. To the executive's chagrin, these notes became part of the hearing. It was awfully tough to

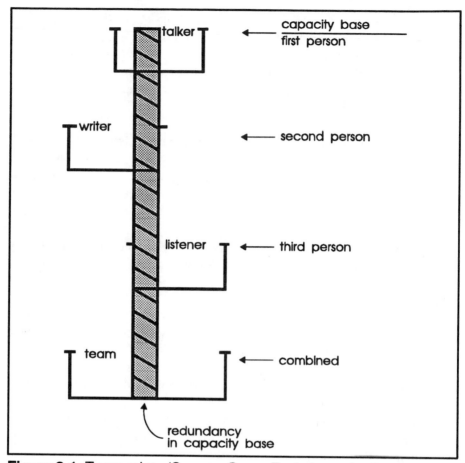

**Figure 3-1.** Team roles. (Source: Group Techniques for Program Planning, A. L. Delbecq, et al.)

recall events of a year ago; to explain precisely what the executive's notes meant during the price negotiation. The notes played a big part in the FTC's success.

The role of writer is passive. Listening is the most critical asset for anyone filling this role. It is always worthwhile to have an extra pen and paper for opponents who may not think to bring them. Opponents should have the same option as negotiators to make a record.

## Example

A three month negotiation dealt with health care rates and costs. The two parties were the former U.S. Department of Health Education and Welfare [HEW] and a state Blue Cross/Blue Shield [BCBS] group. The HEW people did not take notes. The BCBS people did. When negotiations were over, BCBS supplied the documentation for both sides. Objectivity was the BCBS goal. However, when a point was indistinct or open to interpretation, one can conclude the way it was defined.

Listeners monitor the direction of the negotiation. Listeners keep talkers on track. And away from danger areas. A strong sense of anticipation and good organization are required listener skills. Listeners must have prearranged signals with talkers so that a recess or caucus can be initiated. Listeners may need to review something. For example, is the talker straying from objectives inadvertently or on purpose?.

Watching others who are skillful is a proven way to develop negotiating skills. Having subsidiary roles on teams is a starter.

## Team Limits

If teams are such a great idea, why are they not used more often? Five constraints slow the growth of team use.

1. Economic constraint [cost]. It is more expensive to use two or three people than to use one.
2. Availability and choice constraints [time]. It is often tough to get the team together for planning, etc. Team preparation is at the expense of members' regular duties.
3. Coordination restraint [interaction]. It is difficult to get the team members to operate within defined roles. Tight discipline is necessary for smooth interaction. This third factor is particularly vexing. The team's cohesiveness can be destroyed when one member agrees with opponents unilaterally. Another problem crops up often. One member may give the opponent data at the wrong time. Keeping non-talker team members quiet is a major hurdle. Having more than one talker opens up tremendous opportunity for opponents to drive a wedge through a team or position. Yet, expertise of the non-talker team members may be needed for issue support. This is allowable when the team member with the expertise acts as a presenter of specialized information. That member then reassumes a passive role while the talker reasserts the verbal role.
4. Cooperation restraint [status]. It is imprudent to ignore differences in team members organizational rank, especially if they interact in other situations. For instance, a higher ranking individual may not be well

equipped to serve as the talker. However, this person also may be uncomfortable about their personal security. They may place a high importance on status to balance out this security concern. In this case, it is pragmatic to assign them the talker role without regard to skill limits. Opponent perceptions about the talker's organizational rank should not be of concern. Opponents get whatever message is there when they see the team operate.

5. Parity with limits constraint [number]. It is best not to outnumber opponents. A one person opponent might be put off by a negotiator's team. And, experience shows that the minority number in a negotiation is superior in success to the majority number. If numbers are equal on each side, up to three members per team is best. An opponent team might arrive with two members when the negotiator's team has three. It is then worthwhile to reduce the negotiator's team to two. Next best is to have less numerical strength than the other party. If the opponent's team exceeds three, negotiators should be unconcerned. People who bring in masses for their side ask for trouble. They compound the constraints already discussed. They add to them the problem of becoming too confident due to numerical superiority. This overconfidence evaporates when the unmanageability of their larger group is apparent.

Figure 3-2 presents a rating for team effectiveness.

---

**Guideline:** Do in-group bargaining before the negotiation begins. Work with the team members to get everyone on the same track, etc. It is absolutely necessary to get team cohesion and alignment in advance.

---

**Guideline:** Get protocol out of the way with opponents at the start. Who on your team has which role; establish ground rules; etc. There are situations where a team approach is ineffective. For other situations, some negotiation should involve teams and some only each party's key team member. These choices are based on the situation.

---

The next chapter discusses critical errors and how to avoid them.

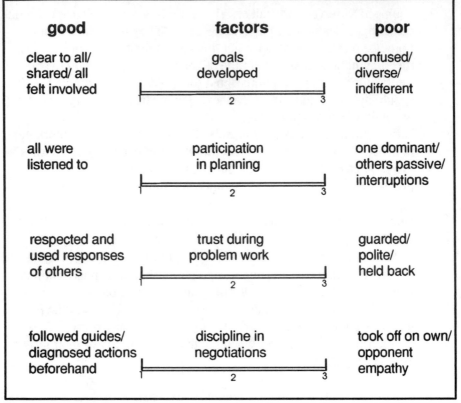

**Figure 3-2.** Rating team effectiveness. (Source: Theories of Group Process, G. L. Cooper.)

# CHAPTER 4

# *THREE CRITICAL ERRORS THAT REDUCE NEGOTIATOR EFFECTIVENESS*

### The Stag at the Pool

*A Stag overpowered by heat came to a spring to drink. Seeing his own shadow reflected in the water, he greatly admired the size and variety of his horns, but felt angry with himself for having such slender and weak feet. While he was thus contemplating himself, a Lion appeared at the pool and crouched to spring upon him. The Stag immediately took to flight, and exerting his utmost speed, as long as the plain was smooth and open, kept himself easily at a safe distance from the Lion. But entering a wood he became entangled by his horns, and the Lion quickly came up to him and caught him. When too late, he thus reproached himself. "Woe is me! How I have deceived myself! These feet which would have saved me I despised, and I gloried in these antlers which have proved my destruction. "*

What is most truly valuable is often underrated.
Aesop's Fables

## Recurring Errors

There are many dos and don'ts regarding negotiating discussed in this book. However, three errors have special importance. They occur often. They may be inherent in the negotiating process.

1. Perspective error is concentrating on the present (now) to the exclusion of the future (later).
2. Understanding error is ignoring built-in differences between negotiators and opponents.
3. Utility error is misvaluing what a negotiator has to trade.

## Perspective

Perspective errors come from over reliance on short term results. Concern for later implications of actions taken and proposals made is insufficient. The difference in attraction between now and later is easy to understand. Figure 4-1 presents reasons for this situation. Being less clear about later should not lead negotiators to build in problems that hurt agreement execution.

Experienced negotiators try to balance now demands in agreements with potential later effects on execution. They ask questions of their strategy. "What is the probable effect of this action on continuing relations with opponents? Is the current situation linked in other ways to our organization, its image, or reputation?" By contrast, people with the win-lose orientation concentrate only on now. They view each negotiation, perhaps each issue, as a single instance. They seldom strike a balance between now and later.

The modifying factor on perspective is that there will only be one agreement with the other party. This condition could affect strategy. Yet, it is difficult to know that the one agreement will not in some way become known to future opponents. Even in single agreements, it is best to act as though the other party will be an opponent again.

## Understanding

Understanding errors result by not identifying important differences between negotiators and opponents. This is excusable only for hidden differences. Subconscious differences are an example. Good prenegotiation planning is a giant step toward minimizing understanding errors. The time to pinpoint important differences is during preparation. These differences, if not dealt with, increase negotiating difficulty. Four of the more important differences and their possible clarifying actions are described next.

1. Unfamiliarity with customs of the industry. Negotiators should know how business is usually conducted in opponent arenas. Likewise, they must discuss the "how" in their own arena.

| Factors Influencing<br>Concentration on Now | Factors Contributing to<br>Avoidance of Later |
|---|---|
| Availability of a resource, often its scarcity. | Poorness of predictability, often tied to unknown or uncontroll able actions changing what looked like a fixed course. |
| Immediacy of a need, often due to schedule or sequence demands. | Certainty of change. It is a given that change will occur. |
| Effect on the negotiator's performance, often related to job evaluation and out put. | Impossibility of measuring just why certain past actions worked. How much was due to luck? How much to skill? |
| More knowns, often due to availabillty of data or access to similar past situations. | Possibility of extras, i.e., more contract clauses, often related to fear about change, increase, availability, etc. |

**Figure 4-1.** Factors pushing attention toward now or away from later. (Source: Sparks Consultants).

## Example

Oil companies generally pay supplier invoices in 90 days. That period can be cut by making arrangements ahead of time. A contractor was doing engineering work for an oil tool manufacturer. At completion, the contractor was not paid in the usual 30 days. Instead, the manufacturer paid the contractor the way in which it received payments from oil companies. The contractor was deficient. It failed to identify the customary payment period in its customer's industry. The contractor incurred interest expense on the money it borrowed waiting for payment. Failures generate penalties.

2. Differences in value definitions. Where values are concerned, negotiators must recognize differences in definition.

## Example

The definition of a fair business action can vary notably between companies in different segments of the same industry. Primary metals producers enjoy larger dollar margins than do companies in the scrap metal business. Scrap metal businesses must cut sharper deals to make a profit. The definition of fair business action is perceived differently by negotiators from these two industry segments.

3. Economic size differences. Negotiators must communicate their company's policy regarding economic differences due to company size. Smaller entities often think larger ones can better absorb certain costs. They may attempt to transfer these costs.

## Example

A large company had a policy of intentionally placing some orders with smaller businesses. The efficiency of the company's purchasing department was audited. The audit revealed out-of-the-ordinary prepayments made to a smaller supplier of specialized electrical controls. The supplier was asked to justify the size of the prepayments. The supplier admitted they were increased by three times the amount needed. The supplier felt the customer could afford to absorb the carrying charges better than it could. While no overcharge was made, the time change in payments was an economic change to the contract.

4. Unfamiliarity with local customs. Negotiators should always find the pace of an opponent's business environment.

## Example

A negotiator meets with an opponent located in Hattiesburg, Mississippi. The negotiator should expect to have a glass of iced tea, exchange pleasantries, etc. before getting down to the issues. This approach would not get far if attempted in the pressured business environment of New York City. Different industries have their own special pace. Banks and insurance companies seemingly crawl along compared to the frenzy at stock or commodity exchanges. But the bond traders in banks and insurance companies are as rushed as any exchange trader.

## Utility

Utility errors are misestimating the worth of what a negotiator has to trade. Its importance to opponents is incorrectly assessed, usually on the low side. The natural tendency is to undervalue what is already had, especially in excess. This may be the most important of the three errors described. It can spell the difference in reaching an equitable agreement.

## Examples

Consider again the larger company trying to spread some business among smaller vendors to help their growth. Smaller vendors are usually less sophisticated. The margin of error tolerated for smaller vendors may be higher than customary. The larger company is undervaluing its importance in helping smaller suppliers. It is not building within them the discipline needed to survive in more competitive situations. And the smaller supplier never appreciates business tenets because it is dependent on its benefactor's largess.

The technologically endowed West does not use its advanced expertise as an economic weapon. Yet, it is in competition with others who want to replace it as the economic leader. It fails to place a high value on the need for its technology by those competitors. Economic concessions are not extracted for the technology transferred. The technology is often free. The same is true for university education in the U.S.A. and U.K. Others send their people to the U.S.A. and U.K. for undergraduate and graduate work. These people pay the same tuition as citizens. In effect, they get the technology [education] at bargain rates.

## The Negotiation Process: Summary

In this part, negotiation is defined by identifying its characteristics. The advantages and limits of using teams are discussed. Errors that typically crop up to impair agreement are described.

The importance of understanding utility is stressed. The value of anything depends on its actual or perceived utility to those who have it or want it. Quite often the value of something to someone is inversely proportional to the amount of it already held or controlled. It is proportional to the effort required to get what is wanted.

This book's next part details planning and preparation steps. These help negotiations succeed and agreements work.

# PART II

# EFFECTIVE PREPARATION

"Proper planning prevents poor performance." The Hon. James Baker, former U.S. Secretary of State, credits his father with educating him on the need for preparation.

## *Effective Preparation: Introduction*

Preparation is pivotal to effective negotiations. Negotiators and opponents have about the same amount of time to prepare. They may not choose to use the time available for preparation. How each spends preparation time influences how the negotiation evolves. And how it concludes. A review of win-lose versus win-win approaches illustrates how emphasis during preparation effects negotiations.

Win-lose proponents counsel spending time arranging the physical setting to convey impressions to others. They suggest such things as:

- placing seating to get a so called power orientation; and
- practicing body movements to send nonverbal messages that are supposed to manipulate others.

This preparation focuses on gimmicks. It seeks an advantage over others with different viewpoints. Other win-lose preparation involves selecting tactics outlined in Chapter 9. The shortcoming in win-lose preparation exceeds its dubious ethical base. It is its assumption that others are easily intimidated. The assumption that other parties are easily manipulated by gimmicks does not prove out in experience. By contrast, win-win proponents use preparation time learning issue merits. They use systematic steps to ensure adequate preparation. Win-win preparation offers the best chance for a balanced agreement. This is its value. When both parties feel they have gained, the agreement is more likely carried through.

The actions examined in this part of the book are necessary whatever negotiation is involved. The level of importance and complexity in a negotiation direct the amount of time given these actions.

# CHAPTER 5

# *PREPARING FOR NEGOTIATIONS*

*The Wild Boar and the Fox*

*A Wild Boar stood under a tree and rubbed his tusks against the trunk. A Fox passing by asked him why he thus sharpened his teeth when there was no danger threatening from either huntsman or hound. He replied "I do it advisedly; for it would never do to have to sharpen my weapons just at the time I ought to be using them.*

Aesop's Fables

## Skill, Not Art

Negotiation preparation is a skill, not an art. As such, it is learnable. Beyond that, it is perfectible. Acceptance of this premise is the start to being a more effective negotiator. By following the principles and methods suggested, negotiators find how to sharpen planning skills. To do this, a negotiator need not change personality. The need, instead, is to select the principles and methods that will work for negotiators. Those that fine-tune their planning technique. That fit their capabilities.

## Estimating

In negotiations, both parties have information that is:

- complete about the other party in some areas;
- incomplete about the other party in some areas; and
- shared with the other party.

Where information is incomplete, negotiators must estimate. Negotiators who plan well, automatically improve their estimating. Proper planning reduces the unknowns in a situation. This narrows the range of chance occurrences that can upset estimates.

## Preparation

Three actions comprise preparing for negotiations.

1. Collecting and organizing data.
2. Settling questions.
3. Reviewing data and aligning position.

Figure 5-1 shows the amount of preparation time usually devoted to each action. It includes adjusting attitude, an action discussed in the next chapter. Of course, before preparation starts, four general questions should be considered.

1. Is this a negotiable situation? The answer to this question is quickly apparent using the triage method from medicine. In an emergency, people are divided into three groups. The first group will survive without help. Likewise, some issues will be settled without negotiation because of changes that are about to happen. The second group will survive if helped. Likewise, some issues need negotiation to be settled correctly. The third group will not survive, cannot be helped. Likewise, some issues are not resolvable through negotiation. Some other way must be used to settle them.
2. Should we do business with this party?
3. Are they trustworthy?
4. Is the timing right for these negotiations?

### Collecting and Organizing Data

Getting data together and into usable form in preparation for negotiations divides into six steps:

1. Assembling facts and assumptions.
2. Dividing data into categories.
3. Establishing settlement ranges.
4. Assigning bargaining methods.
5. Selecting a starting place.
6. Making a matrix.

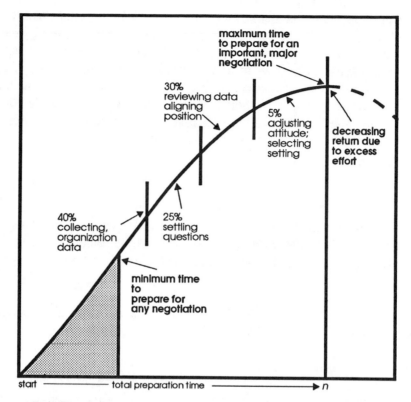

**Figure 5-1.** Times typically spent on each preparation action. (Source: Sparks Consultants).

By doing steps one through five, negotiators have a good chance of being ahead of opponents. Many people are not disciplined enough to get ready right. Doing step six almost ensures negotiators an advantage. Some people cannot conceptually handle this step, though it looks easy. All six steps require little time for a brief negotiation. They might require several days for an important issue. For complex negotiations, like mergers, acquisitions, or with unions, the steps might take several weeks or months.

## Facts and Assumptions

Preparation starts by assembling facts and separating them from assumptions. Facts are data that can be documented. They are non-disputable through support. They should be gathered in one folder or listed on one page. The letter "F" should be entered at the top of all facts. This makes them easily recognized later.

Assumptions are made based on incomplete knowledge. Folders or pages of assumptions should be marked with the letter "A" at their top. This keeps them from being mistaken for or mixed with facts. Nothing is as weak in negotiations as assertions unbacked by facts. If not tracked properly, assumptions might lead a negotiator to accept something as concrete that is clay. Some assumptions are always necessary. Negotiators must judge how much assuming to do in preparation. Some things can be left for development in the negotiation. The best guide to follow is to make only first-level assumptions. Those connected loosely to facts.

## Example

A negotiator assumes no change in the circumstances between an approaching negotiation and those of past negotiations. This session is with the same opponent. It is on the same type issue. The negotiator might conclude that the opponent will do business the same way.

This conclusion is a first-level assumption. It is based on information available to the negotiator. This information is usually:

- past actions of opponents;
- what appears to be similar environmental forces as before; and
- the absence of indicated change in internal policy at opponent organizations.

It is an assumption because changes that alter things might not show until the negotiation.

Second-level assumptions are those connected to other assumptions. They should be avoided.

## Example

A negotiator assumes that the business with an opponent is locked-up before negotiation. For instance, the negotiator   may feel that the opponent cannot walk away or deadlock. The opponent's position is too weak. This conclusion could lead  a negotiator to make inappropriate demands.

That an opponent is locked-up is an example of a second-level assumption. It stems from the untested assessment of opponent position weakness. That assessment is a first-level assumption, however. It is based on the negotiator's information, judgment, and perspective. Negotiators must continually be alert to, and recognize the danger inherent in, second-level assumptions.

## Major and Minor Issues

Dividing facts and assumptions into two categories is next. One category is major issues. The other is minor issues from the negotiator's perspective. By seeing the organizational and factual support for each issue, its value may change and, ultimately, its category. The longer issues of lower importance are dealt with, the greater the chance they get unwarranted status. Issues of lower priority in internal negotiations can be dispatched quickly. Simply put enough high-paid people into the negotiation. Their time value promotes settlement.

## Major and minor issues are separated for two reasons.

1. Negotiators must know ahead of time which of their issues they can be easier about. They decide this using three questions. Which issues are more critical? What potential loss or cost might be incurred to the negotiator's position? How assertive must the negotiator be before becoming easier? In effect, this is a score-keeping mechanism for use in the negotiation. Any issues that end up assessed as non-critical, neither major nor minor, should be excluded. They only serve as gimmicks thrown in to confuse discussion. They falsely complicate issues.
2. Issues should be alphabetized. This avoids tipping off opponents about a negotiator's major-minor distinction. For instance, agendas might be exchanged, as Is customary in union bargaining. An opponent's analysis might be based on a negotiator's first discussion point. Naturally, opponents exert the greatest leverage against a negotiator's major issues. Opponents hope to extract the most concessions possible. Negotiators who spotlight their major points give an unnecessary advantage to opponents.

There is an efficiency based argument against preparing with alphabetized lists. If a negotiator's major issues are not settled up front, the negotiating time may be wasted. These issues might later be found to cause deadlock. This argument gives more weight to efficiency than to effectiveness.

## Settlement Ranges

The third preparation step establishes settlement ranges for issues. These must be expressed in measurable terms. Quantification is best. A second choice is descriptive definition. Figure 5-2 depicts one set of these ranges,

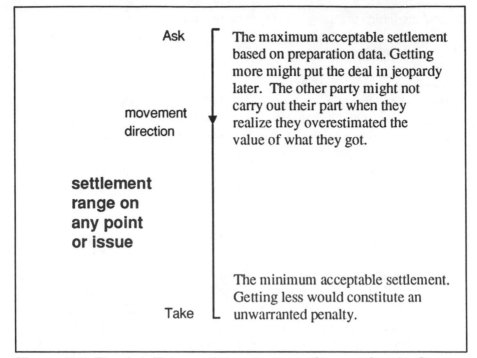

Ask

movement
direction

**settlement
range on
any point
or issue**

Take

The maximum acceptable settlement based on preparation data. Getting more might put the deal in jeopardy later. The other party might not carry out their part when they realize they overestimated the value of what they got.

The minimum acceptable settlement. Getting less would constitute an unwarranted penalty.

**Figure 5-2.** The Ask-Take settlement range. (Source: Sparks Consultants.)

Ask-Take. When proposing a settlement, negotiators begin near the maximum, the Ask point. This is what the negotiator would like if it could be gotten. It must be realistic. Opponents must be able to meet the obligation and complete their part of the agreement to accept the Ask level. If opponents reject the Ask level, negotiators have room to move down the settlement range. This attempts to find a place satisfactory to opponents. If the Take limit is reached and no settlement made, negotiators have a clear stopping place.

When proposing a settlement, negotiators might be making an Offer rather than presenting an Ask. Figure 5-3 depicts the other set of ranges Offer-Give. The Offer is the minimum, the least-fair outlay. It is what the negotiator would like to part with in exchange for what is wanted. This must be reasonable. Opponents must be able to complete their part of the agreement and meet some of their needs to accept the Offer. If rejected, negotiators can advance up the settlement range to find a satisfactory place. If the Give limit is reached without gaining a settlement, negotiators have a clear stopping place.

Correctly prepared ranges make it hard for negotiators to fool themselves into accepting an improper settlement.

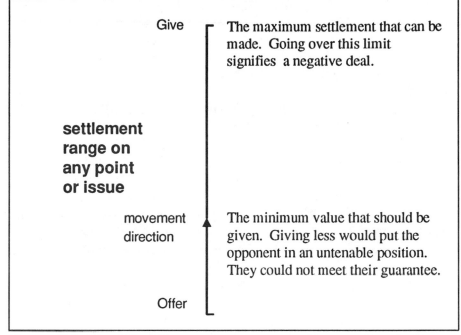

Give — The maximum settlement that can be made. Going over this limit signifies a negative deal.

**settlement range on any point or issue**

movement direction — The minimum value that should be given. Giving less would put the opponent in an untenable position. They could not meet their guarantee.

Offer

**Figure 5-3.** The Offer-Give settlement range. (Source: Sparks Consultants.)

## Example

A maintenance service contractor bid for a major overseas project at one-half the next lowest bidder. This contractor's bid was one-fourth lower than the customer's estimate. The internal estimate showed the minimum needed by a contractor to break-even. The bid was accepted anyway. Halfway through the job, the contractor pulled out. The customer had to pay another contractor a premium to complete the maintenance service. The premium, when added to the original price paid the first contractor, exceeded the next lowest original bid. It was well above the break-even figure developed internally by the customer.

In this example, the purchasing people should have shown the low bidder why they thought its bid erroneous. They should have gotten re-bids. Alternatively, they could have covered the contract with a performance bond. This type of bond is paid for by the contractor. Its cost is added to the price charged the customer.

There is another factor supporting the need for pre-established settlement ranges. People often negotiate toward equity, at least in western cultures.

Settlement ranges help establish equity.  When equity cannot be established, expectations of one or both parties may be unrealistic.  Mis-impressions then exist about what is possible, what is probable, and what is out of the question.  This is a luxury negotiators cannot afford.   Nor can negotiators assume opponents want to or can correctly establish equity.  Negotiators must carefully develop realistic settlement ranges.   However, modification can take place during the work of "Reviewing Data and Aligning Position."   Other changes can occur and be tracked during negotiation.

Settlements reached quickly are usually the result of a gap between the ranges of negotiators and opponents.  This gap is an Offer made that is more than an Ask of the other party.  Or an Ask made that is lower than the Offer of the other party.  Poor preparation by one party is often the cause of the gap.  Quick settlements also may result when both parties are well prepared. They clearly see the equity of Offers or Asks as they effect their positions.

If measurable limits cannot be set for an issue, one of two things is the cause.

1. The issue is really part of another issue.  It is in the wrong form, or is mis-classified.  It should be incorporated with the other issue.
2. The issue is not properly part of the negotiation.  It should be dropped by the negotiator.

## Bargaining Methods

Assigning one of two bargaining methods to each issue is the next step.  The choice of method rests on the:

- dividing issues into major and minor categories; and
- measurement difficulty encountered in finding settlement ranges.

The trade-off method is useful for lower priority issues.  In effect, negotiators swap one issue to opponents to get a different issue from them.  The basis for trade-off bargaining is preferential versus investigative.  Trade-off bargaining is caused by such things as time-limit dictates and issue simplicity.

A caution is in order when considering trade-off bargaining. While the number of issues settled is high, settlement quality may not be part of the outcome.  The more complex the issue, the less it is a candidate for trade-off bargaining. Trade-off bargaining is especially useful for agenda setting at the start of negotiations.

The problem-solving bargaining method is useful for higher priority issues. In effect, negotiators examine an issue's merits with opponents from both their views.  They try to arrive at a solution based on a combination of:

- fact;
- respective merit; and
- the circumstances for each side.

Problem-solving is simultaneously competitive and cooperative. A quality solution is the goal. The output from problem-solving is lower than from trade-off. However, the quality of the settlement is often high. A caution is necessary when considering problem-solving bargaining. It should never be tried without through preparation. It involves intricate moves by both parties. If these moves are unexplored by one party in planning, the settlement probably is lopsided toward the other party. Figure 5-4 describes the steps for problem-solving. Problem-solving helps teams prepare better.

| Sequence | Questions to Answer or Actions Required |
|---|---|
| Clarify the issue(s). | What is the tangible issue? Where do both parties stand? Do they see it the same way? Do they see it of equal importance? |
| Generate and evaluate possible solutions. | Each party identifies what it thinks are practical solutions. Each works with the other to weigh those solutions. |
| Determine the best, not necessarily the ultimate, solution. | This involves settling on the solution most acceptable to both parties. It should have as much merit as possible. It should have results that will last through the life of the agreement. |
| Examine implementation. | Calculate how the solution will be carried out. Identify potential problems. Include steps to deal with them in the agreement, if possible. |

**Figure 5-4.** Problem solving steps. (Source: Clear Thinking, R. W. Jepson.)

Negotiators do not always have an option on the bargaining methods available. Actions within a negotiator's organization may predetermine methods. This situation imposes severe limitations on negotiators.

## Example

The technical people in a multinational manufacturing company excessively rework large project specifications. This is done during project planning. They use most of the total get-ready time. This causes a habitual shortening of procurement time. Procurement does not have time to accomplish all the steps company policy stipulates for selecting suppliers. The result is often a trade-off bargain. The company pays a premium to get delivery of material within project completion schedule limits. Obviously, some vendors are able to decide that, at trade-off bargains, cost is secondary in importance to schedule compliance. Just as obviously, this company's technical people have more internal clout than procurement people. These technical people repeatedly cause policy abortion. There is no penalty to them for that action.

## Starting Position

The fifth preparation step is picking a starting position for negotiation. The position should be headlined by an issue that is likely common to both parties' agendas. This selection keeps the negotiators from divulging agenda issues not on opponents' agendas. If negotiators exposed such issues, opponents gain leverage. Alternatively, the possible starting issue may be randomly chosen. The alphabetized list described under "Major and Minor Issues" also can be used. Opponents will have little or no clue to the importance of a negotiators' issue. They get no pattern to key on. Opponents cannot develop strategy against a predictable approach by negotiators. Opponents must work the issue. That is where negotiator preparation skill pays off.

## The Negotiation Matrix

Look at Figure 5-5. It shows an example matrix. How was it made?

## Example

To make a matrix, start a column heading at the top left side for factors. List the factors. Make a row reading across the top for action options. List the action options. Fill in the effect of action

| FACTORS | GO-IT-ALONE | | JOINT VENTURE | | LICENSE | | SELL OFF | |
|---|---|---|---|---|---|---|---|---|
| | | | | OPTIONS | | | | |
| ROI SIZE . . . . . | most | 5 | good | 4 | some | 3 | low | 2 |
| ROI SPEED . . . . | least | 1 | some | 2 | good | 3 | best | 5 |
| NEED + TIME . . . | most | 1 | some | 2 | little | 3 | low | 5 |
| NEED + $ . . . . . | lots | 1 | some | 2 | little | 4 | none | 5 |
| EFFECT ON REPUTATION . . . | best | 5 | good | 4 | some | 2 | none | 1 |
| FACTOR SUMS . . | 13 | | 14 | | 15 | | 18 | |
| x OPTION WEIGHTS | 1 | | 5 | | 4 | | 2 | |
| = OPTION VALUES | 13 | | 70 | | 60 | | 36 | |

best actions

The points given each F + the weight given each AO are judgments by the assessor.

**Figure 5-5.** A matrix assessing new product strategy (Source: Sparks Consultants.)

options on the factors where the rows and columns join. Use terms like most, best and lots for the high ratings for each effect. Use good, some and little for mid-ratings. Use none, low or least for bottom ratings. Five classifications are enough. Add points to each effect. Use a scale of 5, most effective, to 1, least effective. Sum the factor points for each action option. Set the action options' weights. Multiply the sum of each action option by its weight to get its value.

Making a matrix finds relationships between issues. The matrix is a rectangular array of issues and resources. It makes resources common to two or more issues identifiable. This step lets negotiators avoid a serious problem. They might settle one issue and later discover that the settlement boxed them in on a subsequent issue. The matrix can only be done last. It is choice since sometimes it is unnecessary. A matrix is not helpful if only one issue is being negotiated and its parts have no common resource basis. Mostly, the matrix

| Points | Resources | |
| --- | --- | --- |
| | $ | Delivery Time |
| **Packing** | | |
| loose, unwrapped | 10/doz | 1wk |
| loose, wrapped | 15/doz | 1wk |
| individually wrapped and boxed | 30/doz | 3wks |
| range | 10-30 | 1-3 |
| **Specification** | | |
| .006 tolerance | standard | n/c |
| .004 tolerance | +50/doz | n/c |
| .002 tolerance | +100/doz | 1wk |
| range | 0-100 | 0-1 |
| **Color** | | |
| regular paint | standard | n/c |
| special paint, any two colors | +2/doz | n/c |
| range | 0-2 | 0 |

**Figure 5-6.** A sample single issue negotiating matrix (Source: Sparks Consultants.)

is helpful.  Issues and resources usually have an important interrelationship. Figure 5-6 shows a  matrix for an issue.

## Example

In the matrix in Figure 5-6, the issue is price.  Three points packing, specification, and color  have price implications. They represent a related-by-resource set of points.  Time implications exist for packing and specification, but not for color.  Packing and specification become stronger related-by resource points.  As each point is discussed, negotiators may uncover data from opponents that change their position. Negotiators then decide whether to revise ranges, etc. Assume the total expenditure range available to the buyer in Figure 5-6 was $17 Give to $10 Offer. This automatically excludes the individual boxing option. If loose wrapped is selected, the buyer can pay up to $15/doz and still get special paint at $2/doz. That puts the buyer at the Give limit. Unless specifications are special, the standard of .006 tolerance is acceptable. The buyer should learn if order size affects the packing cost. A large order might be used to reduce cost or get concessions on the paint, etc.

Negotiators use a matrix to see the likely impact of individual settlements on the whole negotiation. The choice can be to make a settlement tentative, based on the outcome of successive, related-by-resource issues. Negotiators may opt instead not to highlight these issue interrelationships. The choice can be to make all settlements tentative, based on final agreement.

## Other Pluses From Matrix Use

Using a matrix has other values. It is the best way to show variables that are subject to control and those that are not. This knowledge is critical. Most negotiations have variables. Variables are part of two problems.

1. Problems of competition. This is having to select strategies without full knowledge of the other side.
2. Problems of allocation. This is having to assign resources among possible uses that exceed total resources.

Most questions negotiators face entail making decisions under conflict conditions. The outcomes from these decisions are unpredictable. Therefore, a negotiator's intuition and judgment play a key role. A matrix, while imperfect, aids in judgments. The matrix is also important because negotiations are not usually zero sum activities. Their outcome is seldom totally one way or one sided. Finally, negotiators can use matrix models when dealing with strategic questions. The models can:

- list payoffs from various strategies available to negotiators and opponents; and
- highlight the strategies that offer the best chance of success.

## Settling Questions

The second planning action is answering questions about negotiation conduct.

1. Are there any possible penalties or alternatives?
2. How can weak points be strengthened?
3. What limits exist?
4. Who supports which issue?

## Penalties and Alternatives

Questions about possible penalties are negatives to a negotiator's side. These are a potential loss or a liability increase. For example, what is the cost if the negotiation ends in stalemate. This helps decide how strong an effort to make to avoid stalemate. The answer includes:

- fixing the out-of-pocket preparation cost;
- looking at alternatives for finding another party to negotiate with;
- maintaining operations and financial position if goals are not achieved; and
- estimating any effect on other relationships with an opponent.

## Example

An aluminum metals manufacturer purchases all the by-product coke produced by several chemical plants. This coke is superior to other coke as a fuel source for converting ore to ingots. It is sought competitively. The chemical plants are a division of a company that has a joint venture in shipping with the aluminum company. Negotiating coke prices with the chemical plants is done at arms length. Even so, actions by the aluminum company negotiators might affect the shipping company joint venture. Actions contemplated by the aluminum company negotiators should include assessing probable impact on that other relationship. Doing otherwise would be naive.

Seeing alternatives to any situation requires looking beyond the obvious. To look past the usual answers that are easily identified. An exercise in finding alternatives illustrates how difficult it can be to uncover them. The exercise is adapted from E. R. Emmet's Learning to Think.

## Example

A table of eight numbers follows. The task is to identify the ninth number(s) for the blank box in the table.

| 4 | 8 | 20 |
| 9 | 3 | 15 |
| 6 | 6 | [  ] |

On investigation, there is no ratio across or down, e.g., no pattern. However, the numbers in the third column are all larger than the sum of the others in their own row. Pursuing this fact further, it can be seen that $4 + (2 \times 8) = 20$, and that $9 + (2 \times 3) = 15$. A rule can be deduced for this table. Adding the number in the first column to twice the number in the second gives the sum in the third. Therefore, the number in the box on the table should be 18: $6 + (2 \times 6)$. Does 18 cover the possibilities? No. There are others. Look down the numbers. The third number in the two columns is the difference between the first and second number and the addition of one $(9 - 4 = 5 + 1 = 6)$ and $(8 - 3 = 5 + 1 = 6)$. Another rule can be deduced for this table. Adding one to the difference of the first two numbers of any column gives a third number. Therefore, the number in the blank space on the table should be 6 $(20 - 15 = 5 + 1 = 6)$. Is 18 preferable to 6 as an answer? There is no way to tell. Judgment comes into play when picking among alternatives. Negotiators must identify alternatives to apply their judgment to the most possibilities.

## Strengthening Points

Another question to address is how to strengthen weak points. A primary option is bluffing. It carries a double risk, however. First, a failed bluff converts to a liability. The liability is an increase in psychological advantage for the other party. This advantage can persist through several subsequent issues. Secondly, failed bluffs reduce trust. The previous level of trust can be difficult to regain. This trust loss can cause protracted negotiations. One party seeks to establish thoroughly the other's real position on each new issue to avoid being bluffed.

Though the double risk is important, some circumstances make bluffing a potential choice. For example, a bluff may be tried when a negotiator has a weak case on a pivotal issue. Also, a bluff may be tried when there are high stakes involved in gaining a pivotal issue.

## Example

In poker, it is foolhardy to bluff in a 5 cents, 10 cents, 25 cents, three-raise-limit game. It is too easy for some player to stay in just

| Design of Opponent Organization | Area(s) of Primary Interest | Typical Conflict Points Due to Organization Design |
|---|---|---|
| Functional [manufacturing based]. | Size of own contributions to success versus other functions'. | Between functional areas. Does opponent represent a dominant function or a lesser function in their organization? |
| Product or service [technology based]. | Growth of own business area. | Between divisions. Is opponent in a growing or shrinking division in their organization? |
| Process [metals, energy, flow based.] | Maintaining operational quality of own segment [technical excellence rules here]. | Between segments. Is opponent in a segment toward the front or more toward the end of the process cycle [end people are often very dependent; sometimes paranoid]? |
| Matrix. | Fluid. | At all levels. |

All designs can exist in one organization. But one predominates. The higher an opponent's job level, the broader their view and the less they sub-optimize. All the conflict points can exist in the same organization. But one will be more critical than the others.

**Figure 5-7.** Seeing internal support available to opponents. (Source: Sparks Consultants).

to see the cards. In table stakes or pot limit poker, a bluff might work because the stakes make a wrong call expensive.

**Guideline:** In deciding whether to try a bluff, never do it unless absolutely necessary. And never tell anyone it worked.

## Limits

Negotiators get insight into boundaries confining their actions by answering the question of what limits exist. These limits include:
- the authority the negotiator has or how far they can go on their own;
- how much money they can commit;
- how critical their say is if they decide to abort the negotiation;
- the number of items that can be discussed in negotiation or how much time is available;
- issues that cause conflict with others if brought up at the same negotiating session; and
- schedule requirements of when the agreement is needed or lead time.

Negotiators can find their situational limits easier than those of their opponents. Most opponent limits found by negotiators are the product of assumptions. Negotiators should confirm their validity as early in negotiations as possible.

## Support

Negotiators get clues to issue importance by answering questions about who supports those issues. It helps in drawing assumptions about the underlying causes of issues. The expectations of others may show the potential support for issues. Part of the how-much-support analysis can be made by looking at the design of opponent organizations. Figure 5-7 presents the usual locus of conflict related to organization design. Apparent issues may not be the real objectives of others.

## Example

A usually reliable supplier of bearings to a tool manufacturer began to miss critical delivery dates. No new element in the relationship could be identified by the manufacturer to justify the service drop-off. Erratic delivery repeated itself a few times. The supplier could offer no assurance of correction. The manufacturer switched to another supplier. Later, the manufacturer discovered that the former supplier had committed almost all its output to a lucrative overseas contract. By having the manufacturer break the relationship, the supplier hoped to avoid an opportunistic reputation. The supplier wanted to leave the door open if it needed the tool manufacturer's business again.

## Reviewing Data and Aligning Position

This third preparation action, in sequence, is:

- review;
- brainstorm;
- test; and
- make a "must" list.

The agenda is ordered during this part of preparation. Issues are positioned so that they are in the best negotiating order. Usually, this is from the general to the specific. This is not the alphabetical agenda negotiators work from during negotiations. It is for getting a perspective to assess the flow of issues.

## Review

This is required. It is a review of two previous actions. Collecting and ordering data, and settling questions. The review focuses on information sufficiency and depth adequacy. Is the material too shallow? Is it unconvincing? The review often has positive results.

1. Getting additional data improves the position support. The value of this data makes the difference between a solid case versus only a good case.
2. Tightening coordination between negotiators and any backup that might be required. This includes any technical presentations by experts who would not be a part of the continuing negotiation meetings.
3. Clearing up any final questions and closing any gaps in team members' knowledge.
4. Smoothing out the mix of information. The more important parts are mixed with less important parts to aid opponent receptivity. An opponent bored or dulled by lack of variety or texture might miss the convincing merits of a negotiator's side.

Chapter 11 discusses the methods for getting a high level of opponent receptivity. Figure 5-8 shows the sequence for data evaluation and disposition.

## Brainstorming

Brainstorming is optional. Brainstorming's purpose is to find creative aspects to the data. These might provide added dimension to a negotiator's position. Its strength might be increased. There are many ways to brainstorm.

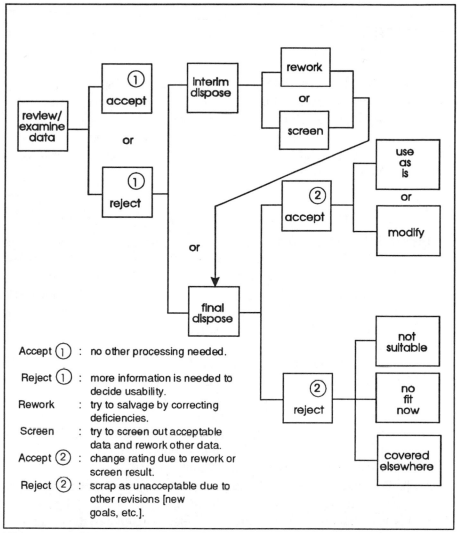

**Figure 5-8.** Ranking and disposing of data. (Source: Sparks Consultants.)

One effective way follows.

1. A group of people sit in a room for usually no more than an hour. They examine a well-defined issue.
2. Each person makes a statement about the issue. They are uninhibited by any rules, and can move in any direction. The statements need no amplification.
3. These statements are recorded without challenge to their validity. De-

tail is not probed. There is no discussion at all.
4. The ideas are reviewed. Any that give previously unthought of weight to a negotiator's position are kept.

Brainstorming does not always produce improvement. Its chance for success depends on accepting the premise that it uncovers creative aspects. There are well-run, successful companies that do not hold with the premise. Brainstorming works well in organizations that foster free-flowing interchange between authority levels. Brainstorming is a useful tool for figuring out how to break stalemates.

## Testing

Testing the strength of positions gets them aligned. This is arduous. And required. This is the chance to fix weaknesses and mistakes at small cost. Opponents correct them for negotiators at greater cost during negotiations. Without testing, the validity of preparation can only be decided during negotiation. That is an unattractive alternative. A well-executed test reduces the potential for disaster. A good way to test follows.

1. Someone takes the opponent role This person is the Devil's Advocate [DA]. DAs should be someone other than negotiators. They should not have been in the preparation effort. It helps if a DA has been exposed to the opponent or their organization. It is very useful if the DA has been opposite the opponent in negotiations. DAs should be supercritical. DAs should not be daunted in the opponent role. A negotiator's organizational superior or peer make good DAs.
2. The DA challenges the negotiator's position when weakness in backup data or hesitancy about facts are uncovered.
3. On-the-spot adjustments are made and incorporated into the negotiator's position. Strategic moves are developed to increase chances for success.

Testing has shortcomings. It cannot duplicate the personal chemistry between negotiators and opponents. Nor will DAs have all the information available to opponents for evaluating various positions.

## "Must" Lists

"Must" lists are required. They are a checklist of data that must be communicated to opponents. These data are needed no matter when a settlement is reached. Without a "must" list, an agreement could omit a critical item. Negotiators then have to contact opponents later and discuss the omitted item. An opponent's response might take any of several unfavorable forms.

1. Refusing to accept that item's inclusion in the agreement. A deal made is a deal to be kept.
2. Reopening the negotiation because the opponent had also inadvertently left out data. The opponent has thought of other issues to discuss.
3. Raising the question of negotiator trustworthiness. "Is this an attempt to slip in something extra?"

The situation can occur where a "must" piece of data is inadvertently left out of an agreement. If that happens, what is the best negotiator approach to the other party? The contact basis should be "Do you remember when we talked about..." not "I forgot to mention...". Negotiators should be prepared to encounter some form of penalty. Opponents will want a quid pro quo to get the "must" item included in an agreement.

## Example

A company temporarily hired a technical specialist to help solve a vexing problem overseas. Some work was to be done in the United States and some on-site. The fee and expenses were negotiated. A contract was signed. The specialist later discovered that a tax on earnings onsite would be due the foreign government. The company did not bring this up in negotiating the fee. The specialist was unfamiliar with tax considerations in overseas work and so did not ask about them. The specialist was able to re-negotiate the contract to include coverage of the overseas tax. But the question of trust had been raised. It created a distance between the specialist and company people. Their relationship was cool and formal.

The "must" list is an under used tool in negotiations.

The next chapter describes how negotiators can set their attitudes to help launch negotiation on a productive course.

# CHAPTER 6

# *ATTITUDE, PHYSICAL SETTING, AND CLOCK TIME*

### The Two Bags

*Every Man, according to an ancient legend, is born into the world with two bags suspended from his neck - a small bag in front full of his neighbor's faults, and a large bag behind filled with his own faults. Hence it is that men are quick to see the faults of others, and yet are often blind to their own failings.*

Aesop's Fables

## Adjusting Attitude

Negotiators should initiate the attitude and mental set that foster successful negotiation.

1. Remove as many self-constructed barriers as possible. Clinging to biases lifts them to obstacles. This is unproductive. Negotiators should review biases toward opponents, even write them on a note pad. This act purges biases temporarily. Negotiators can then work with opponents without mixing in non-negotiating items. Also, it is useful to jot down any feelings that might impair negotiating progress. Afterward, negotiators can reread the list to reinstall the biases.

> **Guideline:** Strive for controlled neutrality toward opponents during negotiation.

2. Avoid having to choose between conflicting personal needs and organizational objectives. Have a strong attachment to organizational goals. Subordinate personal, emotional level, needs. Orientation away from oneself and toward their organization provides negotiators the self-motivation necessary for success. It averts strife between personal and organizational goals.

> **Guideline:** Negotiators who narrow their normal emotional range while in contact with opponents can concentrate on strategy. They stay issue oriented.

3. Create as little stress as possible. The friction accompanying conflict has already been described. It makes a stressful state. There is no need to purposely add stress on opponents. That is counterproductive. Opponents must be receptive for negotiators to get any message across. Openness and relaxation aid receptivity. Stress, on the other hand, creates tension. Defensiveness and lower receptivity follow. Stress also consumes energy better used in gaining viable solutions to conflicts in negotiations. Opponents whose energy is depleted by stress might hole-up. That makes negotiations unnecessarily long.

> **Guideline:** Do not contribute to stresses already present. Of course, negotiators are not responsible for strains self-concocted by opponents.

4. Gain as much understanding of opponent values as possible. Before negotiations, when practical, negotiators should spend time with opponents. This is an opportunity to breed a relationship that aids agreement. Negotiators can use it to reduce barriers by displaying objectivity. They can convey respect for opponent positions. Similarities between negotiators and opponents should be highlighted. They enhance the working relationship of the two parties. Negotiators can help set a professional level and tone for negotiating conduct. They can identify areas of differences unrelated to the negotiations. These should be skirted to avoid ticking-off opponents needlessly. Emanual Kant, the German philosopher, says value can only be assigned to internal things. Like thought and ideas. Kant says value cannot be assigned to external things. Like natural science. Kant is the basis for

the western societal view of idealistic and spiritual concepts that "We can direct ourselves." The eastern societal view is that external things, like fate, play the dominant role in what happens to us.

---

**Guideline:** Be alert to what opponents say in the time before negotiation starts. Interpret those pieces of information that are keys to opponents' personalities. When most people outline things they are doing, they show themselves in the best light possible. They also invariably include trivial particulars about things that mean a great deal to themselves. These slip out unconsciously. They describe a person's real passions.

---

5. Develop as great an understanding as possible of personal limits. Negotiators should review personal habits, quirks, etc. They must become aware of things that can interfere with their ability to negotiate. There are three categories in this awareness:

- mental;
- physical; and
- emotional.

An example of a mental habit harmful in negotiating is wandering attention. The negotiator's inability to concentrate can result in missing a critical concession. A physical constitution can work against effective performance. For example, inability to drink alcoholic beverages in one evening and think clearly the next day. Mental and physical limits are manageable. Wandering attention can be corrected for the negotiating period. Negotiators can consciously direct attention to the subject under discussion. A person can discipline themselves to defer alcoholic intake beyond capacity before negotiating. The emotional category is the problem. Few people can purge private serious concerns, e.g., a loved one seriously ill, being in a tough financial crunch, etc. However, negotiators must leave their losses from a previous negotiation outside a current one. Carrying losses forward to the next negotiation is a sure way to be ineffective. It can help opponents to easy victories.

---

**Guideline:** Know your own mental, physical, and emotional shortcomings. Shore them up whenever they might lessen negotiating effectiveness.

In brief, negotiators must distinguish between two types of involvement - personal and emotional. Personal involvement is necessary for self-motivation. Emotional involvement is a hindrance. It opens the way for impulses to emerge. It is difficult to keep a disciplined approach when impulse dominates.

## A Few Words About Message Sources

There are two classes of messages. Auditory and visual.

## Auditory Messages

Auditory messages are:

- the sound of voice;
- the actual words used; and
- how rapidly the words are spoken.

Auditory sources are valuable during negotiations for finding message meaning. They are also valuable in seeing how strongly senders feel about a message's subject. Chapter 11 discusses techniques for using and receiving auditory messages.

## Visual Messages

Visual messages are:

- the eyes and facial expression;
- the tilt of the head;
- posture;
- movements of the body; and
- appearance.

Of these, the eyes and facial expressions are scientifically documented. There is ample clinical data on the meaning of eye movements and facial expressions. Over twenty years of research has gone into the book Faces. It is used by professionals as an aid in clinical counseling. Psychologist Albert Mehrabian's book, Silent Messages, is a good source. It shows 40% to 50% of a message comes from facial expression and 30% to 40% comes from vocal tone.

Using this data is a problem. It takes time to learn the multiplicity and meaning of facial expression combinations and eye movements. Even if these are learned, some people can mask or control them through training.

The other four visual message sources can be grouped into mostly unresearched and unproven, but popular, "body language." The problem about these sources is the ease with which they can be controlled. The message sources of tilt of the head, posture, and movements of the body are readily manageable. It follows that they are less reliable as measures of people's real intent or message meaning. A person's appearance can result from many things. They may have used an appearance consultant to select the best clothing for a meeting. Their mother may have dressed them. They may be perspiring because of ingesting an antihistamine, not because they are nervous.

---

**Guideline:** Negotiators should pay attention to all three auditory message sources and to eye movements of opponents during negotiations. The question to answer is "Do the facial expression and words tie together?" A person who looks pleased while saying that the deal offered is too tough gives contradictory data. Negotiators process observed data from other visual messages the way they process those data in social situations. Without particular special attention.

---

**Guideline:** Negotiators sometimes deal with opponents from other cultures. Negotiators should first become acquainted with any physical constraints or movements that might be peculiar to those cultures.

---

## A Few Words About Physical Setting

### Negotiation Site

The question of what is a good site for negotiations is overblown. Anthropologists are split about the value of the physical site as to whom comes to whom. Some say going to an opponent's location is a subliminal attack. A negotiator invades opponent territory. Other anthropologists claim it is a surrender to enter opponent territory. For properly prepared negotiators, it makes little difference where the negotiation is held. The exception is where physical limit dictates the location. Examples are the location of a volume of data or a need for site inspection. Negotiators should not be influenced by the location. They realize that having opponents select the sites might remove some opponent stress. A more comfortable opponent is more receptive.

## Example

The negotiator responsible for a large hotel chain's multimillion-dollar acquisition deals designed an office space to help negotiate. There is a generous conversational area, a smaller "close" area, and a formal area for rejecting issues. This person's track record is excellent. Perhaps for them the office setting is important. However, their industry opponents usually command smaller resources. They initiate the visits to this negotiator. When after financing from banks and insurance companies, this negotiator is comfortable visiting their locations. And, is equally successful at getting the financing.

## Layout

Some people claim the table shape effects negotiation. Wrong. They also claim seating effects it. Right. The best research on the effects of seating and table shape is from the University of Wisconsin. The study involved 300 people in conflict situations, usually one versus one. Four seating arrangements were used with different table shapes. The shapes had no significant influence on the outcomes of the conflict exercises. The seating arrangements did. The four arrangements for two negotiators, A and B, are:

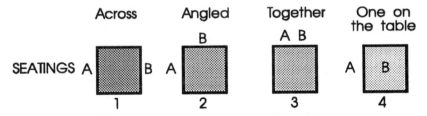

Arrangements 1 and 2 work out best. People are comfortable. They are able to work through their conflicts. Arrangement 3 made people uncomfortable. It added to the conflicts and strained the exercises. Arrangement 4 was done to cover possibilities. It is unlikely negotiators will be met by opponents sitting on a table.

These same arrangements are valid for team seating.

## A Few Words About Clock Time

Each person has an energy cycle. At the high part of this cycle they are more alert. They are apt to do their best. Negotiators should try to schedule negotiations to correspond to the high part of their energy cycles.

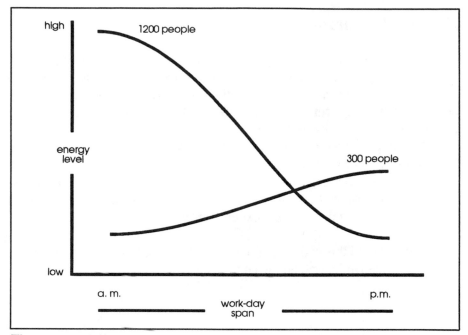

1200 people

energy
level

300 people

low

a. m.

p.m.

work-day
span

**Figure 6-1.** High and low energy trends for 1500 people who negotiate often. (Source: Sparks Consultants.)

Fifteen hundred negotiators attending Sparks' Negotiating Skills Improvement seminars supplied data about their energy cycles. The majority showed
their cycle higher in the morning. Figure 6-1 gives this data.

Negotiators should keep energy cycle in mind when traveling across time
zones. For short periods of travel, negotiating meetings should be arranged to
correspond to the negotiator's customary time zone. The question of jet lag
must be dealt with by some negotiators, not all. Some are able to pump-prime
their energies. They show no noticeable effect from across-time-zone travel.
Michael DeBakey, a heart surgeon, travels extensively. Dr. DeBakey finds
one good way to adjust quickly to another time zone. Fast while traveling to
it. Drink lots of nonalcoholic liquids. Then, eat at the regular meal time in
the new time zone. A person's body automatically adjusts to the new time
zone schedule.

Negotiators should watch the clock at each negotiation session. Without
discernible progress in the first few hours, experience shows little will be
achieved. Under that circumstance, the guide to follow is to recess or resched-
ule that particular session.

## *Effective Preparation: Summary*

Thorough preparation is as important as expertise to successful negotiating. Getting ready right ensures negotiators the strongest possible case. Negotiators hope to gain objectives benefiting their organization. They also must be attentive to the long-term-relationship effects of their actions. And to possible alternatives if negotiation fails.

Before negotiations conclude, negotiators should have thought out the impression to leave with opponents. Why give to chance what can become a strategic benefit affecting future relations with opponents? The last impression should be planned just as are other actions. That impression is often remembered most at the parties' next encounter.

The next part of this book examines actual negotiations with opponents. It looks into what works well and what to avoid.

# PART III

# NEGOTIATIONS
# CONDUCT

"Here comes the orator, with his flood of words and drop of reason." Ben Franklin said this. It is great advice for negotiators. Be economical with words. That helps people understand what is said. It saves time, too.

## Negotiations Conduct: Introduction

Preparing well takes more time than doing negotiations. Five negotiator actions heavily influence success during negotiation.

1. Categorizing conflict correctly.
2. Having adequate self-protection.
3. Finding opponent need orientation.
4. Managing power factors.
5. Gaining a high receptivity level.

Chapters 7 through 11 treat these actions individually.

# CHAPTER 7

# *CONFLICT*

*The Laborer and the Snake*

*A Snake, having made his hole close to the porch of a cottage, inflicted a mortal bite on the Cottager's infant son. Grieving over his loss, the Father resolved to kill the Snake. The next day, when it came out of its hole for food, he took up his axe, but by swinging too hastily, missed its head and cut off only the end of its tail. After some time the Cottager, afraid that the Snake would bite him also, endeavored to make peace, and placed some bread and salt in the hole. The Snake, slightly hissing, said: "There can henceforth be no peace between us; for whenever I see you I shall remember the loss of my tail, and whenever you see me you will be thinking of the death of your son."*

No one truly forgets injuries in the presence of him who caused the injury.
Aesop's Fables

## Correctly Categorizing Conflict

In negotiations conflicts arise. Some are predictable. Some not. The negotiator needs a model to compare different conflicts. Figure 7-1 shows a useful mental model of conflict. Its design is from psychological research on managing group interactions. Negotiators using this model can make two key decisions about a conflict. The first decision classifies conflict based on solvability.

1. Terminal conflict looks impossible to solve by agreement. It is win-lose.
2. Paradoxical conflict is unclear, its work out questionable. It is often

| | conflict type | | | |
|---|---|---|---|---|
| | terminal | paradoxical | contentious | |
| | agreement seems impossible | ? | agreement seems possible | |
| very | | | | high |
| | win-lose | | win-win | |
| issue intensity | | try to move right or to set aside ➡ | | issue importance |
| less | fate | | trade-off | low |

Negotiators taking contentious positions for important issues, finding no progress, eventually go to terminal conflict. Otherwise, they risk stalemate or deadlock.

**Figure 7-1.** A mental model of conflict by type, intensity and issue importance. (Source: Put Offs and Come Ons, A. H. Chapman.)

later found to relate to an issue out of order. It might have been poorly defined. Or it might be part of another issue, and should not be examined separately. It is neither win-lose nor win-win.
3. Contentious conflict appears solvable. It is win-win.

The second decision classifies conflict based on intensity.

I. Very intense conflicts exist when the issues are highly important to negotiators and opponents. Both are energetic and active in this situation.
2. Less intense conflicts exist when the issues are less important to negotiators and opponents. Both are moderately energetic in this situation. An offshoot of this is when only one party does not care strongly about the issue being negotiated.

Disciplined negotiators make both decisions before reacting to a conflict. Otherwise, they risk acting incompatibly with either the solvability or intensity of the conflict.

## Examples

Finding oneself incontrovertibly locked in a win-lose struggle over a minor point is a failure to classify intensity.

Becoming mired in a debate that offers no possibility of useful outcome is a failure to classify solvability.

These examples do not apply to union-management bargaining. In collective bargaining, intense conflicts are often artificially created over inconsequential points. This is a diversion. Or it is a try at wearing down the other party. Or it is an attempt by union representatives to prove their worth to the bargaining unit. Or it is to delay settlement until the "proper" amount of time has elapsed. Often, collective bargaining lacks the reality available in other negotiations. Collective bargaining often has a scenario that must take place despite the actual amount of conflict between parties.

## Actions and Outcomes by Conflict Type and Intensity

### Terminal Conflict

Terminal conflict involving a highly important point generates win-lose actions by one or both parties. The following is a list of typical win-lose actions.

1. Embracing one's own position as praiseworthy. This becomes especially critical when people believe their position is the only one possible. Simultaneously with downgrading the other party's position, a person's judgment is distorted. Objectivity is lost.
2. Attacking or counterattacking the other party by belittling their position. This casts doubt on its validity. This is followed by showing it inferior to the attacker's position. Conflict increases. Suspicion and subjectivity are promoted.
3. Developing a negative stereotype of the other party. This further provokes them. Respect and confidence in the other party erode.

Terminal conflict distorts a person's ability to think clearly about and understand conflict.  Perspective is difficult to keep.  Actions become incomprehensible as the win motive overwhelms logic and reason.  Commonalities in the parties' positions are minimized.  Their differences highlighted.

The outcome of a win-lose battle is predictable.  One party is the victor.  One the defeated.  Both are marred.  The chance subsequent issues will be handled in a mutually beneficial way is reduced.  Any agreements reached probably will not be genuinely supported by both parties.  A win-lose battle has three results.

1. Competitive feelings and mutually disparaging attitudes become ingrained.
2. Perception of good intentions from either party is blocked.
3. Antagonism, hostility, and distrust are reinforced.

Terminal conflict over a minor point involves actions relying on fate by one or both parties.

1. Avoidance is using any chance mechanism, like coin tossing, to pick a decision.  This evades fighting it out.  Yet, reaching a settlement some way other than chance might be seen as a loss of face.
2. Delay is using any continuance mechanism, such as "not now, but later," to defer a decision.  This reschedules the issue or puts it into limbo.

Fate avoids bloodletting.  Yet, the merits of the issue only contribute to the decision by chance.  When more facts are known, fate may not turn out to be a better choice than other methods.  Its use can produce greater difficulties than first met.

## Paradoxical Conflict

The set-aside method described in Chapter 2 is the best way to handle paradoxical conflict.  Its use lets the parties go to other issues.  They temporarily isolate an issue through neutrality.  The set-aside allows both parties to keep their independence until later.  They may even conclude that mutual indifference is best for the issue in question.

## Contentious Conflict

Contentious conflict involving a highly important issue promotes win-win actions by one or both parties.  The following is a list of typical win-win actions.

1. Feeling optimistic toward oneself and the other party. Understanding and respect for the other party's positions emerge. A collaborative climate results. This does not reduce competitive drives.
2. Clarifying the issue through definition. This emphasizes issue resolution based on the merits of each party's position. It avoids accommodation.
3. Exploring what the facts are and agreeing on these. This develops a range of possible settlements. It avoids the either-one-answer-or-deadlock approach.
4. Reaching agreement by both parties contesting each other's positions. While acceptable to both parties, the agreement is likely not of equal value to both. It is practical.

The outcome of a win-win collaboration is predictable. Both sides achieve at least some of their objectives. A win-win collaboration has three results.

1. Commitment to a genuinely sound agreement gained by mutual effort.
2. Creation of a base for working together in the future.
3. Strengthening of trust by the parties in each another.

The contentious conflict of less intensity involves trade-off actions by one or both parties.

1. Swap is splitting the difference between the positions. Both parties consciously adjust their positions to avoid stalemate. Another form of swap is intentionally exchanging one issue for another.
2. Deprivation is giving up part of a person's resource roughly equal to the resource amount yielded by the other party. A partial loss is preferable occasionally. Nonagreement may mean a total loss. Deprivation also occurs when the parties know that lingering debate costs more than settlement. Formerly unacceptable change to both parties' positions are accepted.

Trade-off's outcome is an acceptable agreement, not always a better agreement. This relieves tension. But the harmony kept is only on the surface. One or both parties may be uncommitted or dissatisfied.

The next chapter discusses protection from intimidation.

# CHAPTER 8

# *INTIMIDATION AND PROTECTION*

## The Fawn and His Mother

*A young Fawn once said to his Mother, "You are larger than a dog, and swifter, and more used to running, and you have your horns as a defense; why, then 0 Mother! do the hounds frighten you so?" She smiled and said: "I know full well my son, that all you say is true, I have the advantages you mention, but when I hear even the bark of a single dog I feel ready to faint, and fly away as fast as I can. "*

No arguments will give courage to the coward.
Aesop's Fables

## Bolstering Resolve

Any negotiator can be intimidated in the right circumstances. The source of the intimidation may be an opponent or a situation. More often it is within a person's mind. It makes sense to take steps that reduce the chance of intimidation. Two steps bolster resolve. They retard being overawed or cowed.

First, form a positive self-image as a negotiator. Self-image is a person's idea of their role in a situation. It is the aware part of personality derived from contacts with reality. It directs a person's self-esteem, e.g., what they think about themself. A positive self-image empowers negotiators to withstand strains inherent in the negotiating process. It lets them balance risks against possible losses. It helps them view change and stay on course. Nervous people, worriers, are unable to keep a positive self-image.

Along with keeping a positive self-image, negotiators need to be goal committed. Emphasizing the rightness of sticking with a valued belief or idea helps commitment. Negotiators who merge their own interests and organizational negotiating goals are hard to dislodge through intimidation. The merger doesn't require emotional involvement. It does require personal involvement. Personal involvement is a cornerstone for a high level of motivation.

Second, negotiators should enact external governances. These are protective limits to negotiating actions. Their format is policies or guidelines. They may be the need for higher authority approval before negotiators can make position changes. Or, they may be limits on accepting other than present objectives. Or, they may specify restrictions on going outside usual terms and conditions.

Developing a positive self-image is the more useful of these two steps. Fears are often self-induced. They have their roots in emotional conflict. They are sometimes self-fulfilling. As Job said, "Hardly have I entertained a fear that it comes to pass and all the evils I foresee descend on my head."

## Private-Versus Public-Sector Protective Limits

The tightness of external governance on negotiators is very different between the private and public sectors, although similar in design. External governance in the private sector is more amenable to change. It is organizational-policy based. The authority to change that policy is readily identifiable. In the private sector, policies generally have the objective of supporting what is to be produced by the organization. They are function oriented.

## Example

A machine-tool company had a purchasing policy forbidding progress payments. Executives let purchasing people ignore the policy in some cases. For example, purchasing people violated the policy whenever that action helped reduce the cost of a purchased component. These progress payments were always calculated on a per cent completion of order; never by date. In effect they reduced the interest cost of the vendor. The vendor passed that saving on to the company.

In the public sector, external governance is tied to administrative procedure. The basis is interpretation of legal checks and standards. The authority to authorize or make changes is often far removed from those doing the work.

In the public sector, the objective of policies is support for how something is done. They are process oriented. Prohibitive external governance hampers intimidation. It also inhibits creative solutions. These are the very solutions by which both parties gain more than originally thought possible.

---

**Guideline:** When negotiating with regulatory agencies and other governmental bodies, first identify what forces dominate them. For instance: Is it a consumer group? Is it the industry being regulated? With the perspective of which constituency is served, the decision process of the agency can be tracked. Strategies can be selected that are appropriate to influencing that decision process.

---

## Understanding Commercial Contracts

The use of commercial contracts is increasing in all types of business negotiations. Commercial contracts can be intimidating for those not trained in legal matters. Negotiators must know the basic elements of commercial contracts. They can then identify when to use experts with legal training. The primary elements of commercial contracts divide into terms or clauses.

### Terms Or Clauses

1. A contract is a written document embodying a particular transaction, agreement, etc.
2. A buyer is the purchaser or user.
3. A seller is the vendor or supplier.
4. A provision is a substantive matter; provisions are sometimes called "terms."
5. A breach is an obligation that has not been carried out due to the fault of either or both parties.
6. A stipulation describes the product or service to be provided by a vendor and the price to be paid by the buyer.
7. A contingency is a happening that might arise during performance of the contract owing to foreseeable or unforeseeable changes in circumstances.
8. A master form contains all elements of a transaction in a single document detailing the vendor's total responsibility for a particular situation.

9. Separately enforceable documents divide various contract elements into phases of the transaction.
10. A master form with amendments reflects changes to the master form decided during negotiations. It must not predate the master agreement.
11. A force majeure is an event that relieves all parties of responsibility for carrying out the agreement. These events should be spelled out.
12. A zipper clause says that all agreements are in the agreement and no other elaborations are needed.
13. A most-favored-nations clause obligates the parties to pass on benefits to one another that are no less favorable than those given to others.

## Coverage

1. Amendments should be in writing. Negotiators should avoid spoken agreements or modifications to written agreements.
2. Warranties should be clear. Implied or expressed warranties should be described in the same words.
3. Assignments of rights under the contract should be limited or forbidden. Non-assignability without written permission is the rule and, then, the assigning party should not be relieved of its responsibilities.
4. Authority of signers to obligate their organizations should be stated.
5. Seller's business should be covered. But if the seller or buyer goes into bankruptcy, the agreement of both parties ends.
6. Compliance with government regulations should be required. A statement should be included that holds the buyer harmless if the seller fails to comply with applicable laws.
7. Confidentiality and non-disclosure of material and information should be protected from third parties. This includes written and unwritten data.
8. Indemnification should be stipulated. Ensuring the correct language requires a legal opinion.
9. Limitation of liability should be stated in money, percent, or other specific.
10. Notices should be described by the method in which they are to be transmitted. This should include designation of who is to receive them and in what format.
11. Survival beyond completion of the contract should include those contract parts as necessary, such as confidentiality. Each contract part should be referenced for specific provisions that survive contract completion.
12. Waivers are where any party relinquishes its enforcement right of a

specific contract part. Waivers should be stated not to void, waive, or modify any other terms or conditions or to relinquish subsequent performance on such items.

13. Patent, trademark, and corporate indemnity should be provided by seller. This should include all expenses that might be sustained, whether an infringement claim against the seller is successful.

Negotiators should remember that the substance of a commercial contract is the primary concern, not the forms used. Compliance with the Uniform Commercial Code is important. A legal review of any commercial contract ensures this compliance.

The use of legal experts in commercial contract evaluation must be separate from their general use as advisors. Negotiators should answer the question "Do I need the legal expert for unique knowledge, or as a general advisor?"

The advent of computer software for contracts is helpful. Negotiators selecting contract software must be sure it meets their need. Using too much formatted data in contracts can set up a bad deal. This usually results from not editing the formatted data to ensure it applies to the agreement.

---

**Guideline:** It is often best to use experts, legal and otherwise, mainly for their specialized knowledge. For other negotiating needs, such as strategic decisions, negotiators should rely on three things. These are common sense, the objective sought, and a person's experiences.

---

**Guideline:** Notwithstanding a commercial contract, negotiators should check on the other parties' past performance or record. Do they and their organization deliver as advertised? Do they and their organization live up to agreements?

---

## Evaluating Visuals

Visual data such as charts, graphs, and pictures suggest a level of objectivity that may be intimidating. Negotiators should examine visual data provided by opponents to ensure that it is not quasi-quantitative. Most visual data are a sample of the total data they purport to represent. All samples have built-in biases. To uncover these biases, negotiators should use five checks.

1. Always check pictures. Differences represented in pictures are often out of proportion to make a greater impact on the viewer.

## Example

□ X has grown by twice as much.  But the picture shows X at four times, rather than twice as much as its former self.

2. Always check charts and graphs to ensure they use the same units horizontally as vertically.

## Example

The diagonal line in the first drawing is twice as steep as in the second. In the first drawing the vertical lines are closer together than the horizontal lines.

3. Always check completeness. Cutting out the middle of a chart makes the differences between compared items visually greater than actual.

## Example

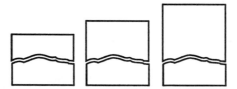

Without knowing the total column height, the importance of the difference between the columns cannot be seen.

4. Always check the term "average". Is it the mean (arithmetic) average, or the median (mid point), or the mode (most frequently occurring)? The median usually tells most about a situation.

5. Always check to be sure tables and charts have scales where needed.

---

**Guideline:** Ask these critical questions about visual data.
1. Is the source genuine?
2. Is the sample large enough to be reliable?
3. Are raw figures used or have percentages been substituted?  If the latter, do they alter the emphasis of the data?
4. Does it make sense?

---

The next chapter describes opponent need orientation.

# CHAPTER 9

# *OPPONENT NEEDS*

### The Peasant and the Apple Tree

*A Peasant had in his garden an Apple Tree which bore no fruit but only served as a harbor for the sparrows and grasshoppers. He resolved to cut it down, and taking his axe in his hand, made a bold stroke at its roots. The grasshoppers and sparrows entreated him not to cut down the tree that sheltered them, but to spare it, and they would sing to him and lighten his labors. He paid no attention to their requests, but hit the tree a second and third blow with his axe. When he reached the hollow of the tree, he found a hive full of honey. Having tasted the honeycomb, he threw down his axe, and looking on the tree as sacred, took great care of it.*

Self-interest alone moves some men.
Aesop's Fables

## Need Theory

The research of Abraham Maslow provides much of the base for current need theory. Maslow closely observed disturbed people. Their distinct behaviors were unburdened by societal constraints. Maslow's conclusions convert to a behavioral theory. A conclusion useful to negotiators is that opponent needs influence style, actions and receptivity to negotiators' positions. People have needs in all the areas described in this chapter. Some needs dominate at one time, others at another time. It is not simple nor easy to uncover and mark people's need orientation. Negotiators wanting more success must develop the skills to analyze opponent needs.

## Identifying Opponent Need Orientation

Finding an opponent's dominant need orientation enables negotiators to work better with them. The first opportunity for negotiators to identify opponent need orientation is before negotiation starts. Next, negotiators should be alert for keys to opponent need orientation during negotiation. Opponents have four basic need orientations.

1. *Low risk.* This is an overriding concern with protection against threat or danger to a person's position, or for the safety of their objectives. Negotiators identifying low risk as a dominant opponent need emphasize certainty aspects of their positions. These lower the risk in an agreement. Negotiators do not need to create, suggest, or imply what is not there. Almost any position has some elements of certainty. Negotiators simply spend more time on these. Other aspects of the proposed solution get less time. Negotiators try to describe things in terms acceptable to opponents.
2. *Association.* This is preoccupation with engaging in social interaction with others, including negotiators. Acceptance by others is crucial to this opponent. Negotiators must make it absolutely clear that the opponent is well regarded and accepted. Emphasizing areas of commonality in both positions is important. This conveys feelings of belonging, sharing, and, ultimately, mutual acceptability to opponents. Negotiators also should emphasize areas personally shared with this opponent. These are like job specialties, interests, ideas, and experiences. This reenforces the relationship. Negotiators should steer clear of commenting on areas where opponents express negative feelings and opinions. Agreeing with opponents that certain things are awful builds no bridge with them. All negotiators do is confirm that opponents are right in their criticism. Negotiators get no credit for that from opponents. Also, such agreement means using a negative talking pattern. Chapter 11 describes the results of this pattern. They are not desirable.
3. *Recognition.* This is the strong drive for personal status. Opponents having a strong recognition need are concerned that others perceive them correctly. They want to be seen in the same vein as they see themselves. Negotiators dwell heavily on aspects of their position that benefit opponent stature or organization. That is the opponent's interest. Identifying a gain for both an opponent and their organization gives negotiators the best chance for a favorable reaction. Status is important to opponents with this need orientation. Negotiators whose titles convey lower organizational status than opponents find

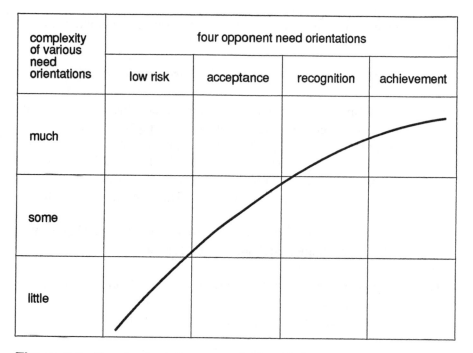

| complexity of various need orientations | four opponent need orientations | | | |
|---|---|---|---|---|
| | low risk | acceptance | recognition | achievement |
| much | | | | |
| some | | | | |
| little | | | | |

**Figure 9-1.** Need orientation complexity. (Adapted from A. Maslow.)

tough sledding.

4. *Achievement.* This is accomplishing tasks in a context that permits the action to serve itself. This opponent is at the other end of the spectrum from one who is low risk. The creative and breaking-new-ground aspects of the negotiator's position are highlighted.

Maslow denoted a basic need level. It is below low risk. It involves concern for food and shelter. This need is unlikely to be met in negotiation. Opponents with such a basic need orientation would be in too weak a position. They could not resist much. The lower level the need orientation, the less complex it is. Figure 9-1 shows this. Hypothetically, it should be less difficult to influence low risk oriented opponents. Actuality, need orientation complexity is a minor factor on the influence scene. The style that emerges from need orientation is a major factor deciding the difficulty in influencing opponents. Chapter 12 describes and explores styles in detail.

## Four Common Wants

All parties in negotiations want things beyond meeting their need orientation and reaching their organizational objectives. As a minimum, negotiators should avoid committing an error on any of peoples' common wants in negotiations.

## Ways in which most people want to be thought of by others.

1. Fair.  Accepting, not questioning a person's intellectual honesty or motives.  Where evidence is clear to the contrary, negotiators tighten their procedures.  They might bring in another person to witness what is done.  They would introduce this person as a new requirement of their organization. Questioning opponent honesty directly has little value.  No one is dishonest in their mind.  They are only doing what is necessary.
2. Competent.  Down playing opponent errors rather than causing them to lose face.  Simultaneously, not being gratuitous.

Helping opponents understand something is better than criticizing their failure to understand.  Negotiators might say "I had trouble with this idea until someone gave me more information.  Let me share it with you."

## Things most people want to experience when dealing with others.

3. Stability.  Alerting opponents to changes instead of springing these on them.  Not destabilizing a situation on purpose.  Surprised opponents seldom look at the prospect that they are poorly prepared.  They are embarrassed. Therefore, they seek to blame someone else's actions.
4. Control.  Involving opponents in developing outcomes, not discounting them as contributors.  Treating opponents as equals.  Opponents who actively examine and contribute to possible solutions buy into results.  Those who have solutions given them, even when accepting, do not support results the same.

Support for the existence of these common wants comes from the work of Darwin and Huxley.  They stated the psychological drivers people have.  Each driver is like a captain of a persons's ship.  Usually, one driver is on duty, e.g., dominant, at a time.  If two or more drivers are fighting for control, a person is unable to keep focus.  That person is in disarray.  They cannot be negotiated with until one captain takes control.  The drivers are:

- greed [relates to control];
- pride [connects to competence];

- security [links to stability]; and
- continuance [spans to fairness].

Greed and pride in particular are problems. They continuously override reason. They often cause agreements that fall apart later. In a greed example, people make deals that "are too good to be true". These usually have an economic factor that cannot be passed up. Later, it turns out that the economics of the deal make it unworkable. The great economic advantage disappears. In a pride example, a person sees great personal advantage accruing to themself. Their career or reputation will soar from making a deal. Later, the advantages to the other side lead to a different result for that person's career.

Disciplined negotiators remain alert to opponent needs.

## The Ben Franklin Appeal

How is the appeal to need orientation made? An excellent illustration is the precept Ben Franklin used to attend to  opponent needs. It is simple. It is straightforward. Franklin always presented proposals in strong terms of what they had for opponent interests. Franklin cited real benefits that would accrue to opponents. Opponents by that had reason for going along with Franklin's proposal. Obviously, Franklin's primary reason was that the proposal was in Franklin's side's interest. Franklin did not explore this facet. Instead, Franklin focused on forthcoming opponent benefits. Franklin put proposals in terms opponents found familiar and comfortable. This gave Franklin's proposal added dimension. It gained in meaning.

## Example

As American colonists battled the British, they needed more resources than they could garner on their own. Envoys went to all the European countries asking for money, war materials, ships, and even troops. All these envoys failed, except Franklin. Franklin convinced the French to help. Franklin's argument was not based on the ethical or moral righteousness of the colonists' stand. It was not predicated on the fact that the colonists were losing. Or that their effort was likely doomed without substantial outside aid. Franklin knew sympathy seldom converted to deed.  Instead, Franklin harped on the result of French defeats by the British in Europe and elsewhere. Franklin pushed the idea that British actions caused France's reduced status in the eyes of other governments. Franklin implied, but let the French conclude, they could never get the recognition they wanted with England dominant.  Finally,

Franklin pointed out that British defeat by the colonists would reduce general British prestige and position. The clear inference was that France was the best candidate to benefit from British loss. France would automatically fill any void left by the British.

The need orientation Franklin perceived as strong enough to get the French to act was recognition. It was expressed as pride. Franklin won out by concentrating on the possibility that a single undertaking could regain national pride. It also would elevate France's world-power position. Of course, Franklin's real purpose had nothing to do with the potential benefits to France. Figure 9-2 presents the Franklin model.

---

### Expressed rationale for an opponent's accepting a negotiator's proposal.

*"It is in your own and your organization's best interest to accept."*

| Examples: | Dominant Need of Opponent Who Receives Appeal |
|---|---|
| Situation warrants this outcome. | Achievement |
| Gives you competitive edge. | Recognition |
| Everyone like us is doing it. | Acceptance |
| Safe as the rock of Gibraltar. | Low risk |

**Unexpressed rationale for a negotiator's proposal.**

It is in our own best interest to have this accepted.

| Examples: | Dominant Need of Negotiator Who Makes Statement |
|---|---|
| Meets our objectives. | Achievement |
| Will be well perceived. | Recognition |
| Let us join the group. | Acceptance |
| We give up the least this way. | Low risk |

**Figure 9-2.** The Franklin model. (Source: Sparks Consultants.)

## Job Conditioning

There is an another factor to consider when sizing up opponent needs. Most people do other work besides negotiating. This other work results in what can be called job conditioning. There are a set of demands for success in any job. These demands give the job holder a propensity for certainty or uncertainty.

People oriented to certainty look for propositions having benefits now. That attracts them. They are more interested in absolutes. Typically, these are people trained in valuative disciplines like accounting and engineering. Similarly, they might have jobs requiring them to meet tight specifications or having exacting standards. Examples are maintaining aircraft, running patient tests in a hospital laboratory, and making close-tolerance machined parts.

People not concerned with certainty generally look for and are attracted more to benefits later proposals. They like exploring unchartered areas. These people are often trained in analytical disciplines like sales and law. Similarly, they might have jobs requiring being comfortable with ambiguities and getting along in less structured situations. Examples are brokering commodities, doing research chemistry, and designing prototypes for appliances.

Negotiators must evaluate opponent job conditioning. Then the benefits now or the benefits later aspects in the negotiator's position are emphasized. Doing so betters chances of not turning off opponents.

Using a compatible frame of reference does not challenge opponents mentally to change environments. Figure 9-3 shows the job-conditioning model.

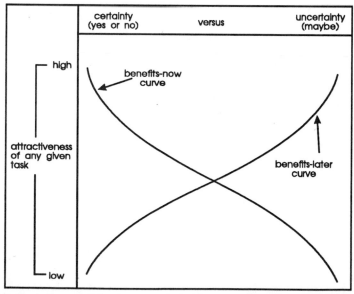

**Figure 9-3.** Job conditioning model. (Source: Psychology of Communication and Persuasion, J. K. Hovland.)

> **Guideline:** Discover early an opponent's regular assignment and training. If possible, identify how the opponent fits in to the formal and informal organizations. Assess the opponent's position in the power structure.

## Control Conditioning

It is important to learn early if an opponent is in a control position in their job. The question to answer is "Does this person own or direct capital?" If they do, they are in a control position. They are more seasoned by having this responsibility.

They will focus more on results and the larger picture than on methods. If not, they may be more concerned with minutiae, with trifles. They are circumspect and less flexible. Method is probably more significant to them than result.

The important role of power is the subject of the next chapter.

# CHAPTER 10

# *POWER*

### The Lion and the Mouse

*A Lion was awakened from sleep by a Mouse running over his face. Rising up angrily, he caught him and was about to kill him, when the Mouse piteously entreated saying: "If you would only spare my life, I would be sure to repay your kindness. The Lion laughed and let him go. It happened shortly after this that the Lion was caught by some hunters, who bound him by strong ropes to the ground. The Mouse recognizing his roar, came up, gnawed the ropes with his teeth, and set him free, exclaiming: "You ridiculed the idea of my ever being able to help you, not expecting to receive from me any repayment of your favor; but now you know that it is possible for even a Mouse to confer benefits on a Lion."*

Aesop's Fables

## Managing Power

Power is always present in negotiating situations. Its value ranges from preeminent to significant. To act competently, negotiators must understand power. They must be able to modify imbalances that favor opponents. What is power? What are its characteristics? What alters the balance of power between two opposing sides?

## Complete Power

Complete power shows itself in several forms. It is the:

- force permitting the imposition of one position over another, no matter their relative merits;
- ability to exert a person's will over others, despite their rank or authority; and
- capacity to influence others to do what they might not ordinarily do in absence of that influence.

The outcome of using complete power favors the party exerting it. However, people who use power intimidatingly while aggressively pursuing their goals often burn the candle at both ends. They forge agreements that do not hold up when the pressure is removed. They create hostility in the other party.

Complete power is rarely found in negotiations. If it existed, there probably would be no need for a negotiation. Negotiators can expect to find a state of incomplete power between themselves and opponents. On some issues one party usually has more strength than the other and vice versa.

## The Six Tasks

In the quest to manage power, negotiators must:

- recognize power discrepancy;
- modify imbalances;
- recognize risk;
- avoid power-based arguments;
- avoid manipulation; and
- use logic tools.

Once understood, these things can be done in ways helpful to the negotiating process.

## Recognizing Power Discrepancy

Negotiators must recognize the amount of discrepancy in power between themselves and opponents. This discrepancy can surpass positional strengths and skill-level differences. Power discrepancy is difficult to find by direct analysis. It is easier to look for the inverse relationship. That is dependency. Dependency is created four ways.

1. *Position.* The reliance on or need of output from another person to complete one's tasks or reach one's goals. For example, the opponent needs the negotiator to do a deal and vice versa. Position dependency is always present in negotiations. The parties' alternatives and ability to pursue them modifies position dependency.

2. *Authority.* The reliance on the authorization or support of another person to move ahead on a project. For instance, a negotiator and opponent must agree to proceed from one issue to another. Authority dependency is always present in negotiations.

3. *Knowledge.* The reliance on another person for information required for one's own needs, work, goals, satisfaction, etc. For instance, by furnishing data not previously known by a negotiator, an opponent confirms as fact what was assumption. Usually, knowledge dependency is present in negotiations.

4. *Affection.* Actual or imposed self-limits on the sources open to fill a person's self-esteem needs. For example, an opponent seeks compliments from a negotiator. Affection dependency is sometimes present in negotiations.

Negotiators finding the dependency situation automatically find the reciprocal: the extent of the power discrepancy. Figure 10-1 illustrates a typical dependency-power relationship.

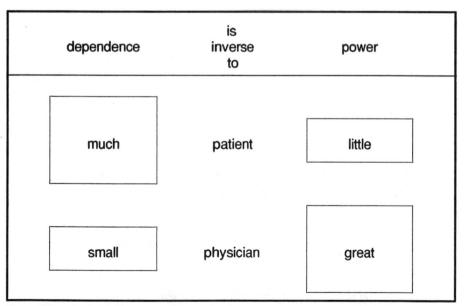

**Example:** A physician has position, authority, and knowledge vastly exceeding a patient's. This is their typical relationship. It is very unbalanced.

**Figure 10-1.** The dependence/power relationship. (Source: Management and Machiavelli, A. Jay.)

## Modifying Power Imbalances

Negotiators must modify existing negative imbalances in power between themselves and opponents.  A negative imbalance is when an opponent's power advantage is based on a negotiator's dependency.  When a negotiator has the advantage, that is the opponent's problem.  Once power imbalance is modified, the merits of each side's position are more important.  A negotiator's thorough get ready then yields real strength.  If the opponent is also well prepared, the negotiation progresses rapidly.  However, observation of many negotiations shows that some people try purposely to create a power imbalance in their favor.  They feel this is a sure means for reaching their goals.

Four broad changes modify an existing imbalance of power in negotiations.

1. Change the authority one or both parties have to make agreements.

### Examples

Expand or contract the settlement range open to either party. They may need to refer more or less often to higher authority. Change the organizational status and title of either party. This may bring the parties closer to positional parity.

Bring in new people to replace those in the negotiation. This has the potential difficulties in information transfer [Chapter 2] and those of adequate preparation [Chapter 5].

2. Change the agenda.

### Examples

Reduce the number or types of items that can be negotiated.
Mutually agree to extend the negotiation to issues not originally scheduled.
Get an item included for which the other party is unprepared.
Cosmetic changes, such as recasting the same issues in different form, are not agenda changes.

3. Change the beliefs about or emphasis on the opponent.

### Example

Negotiators must understand that their positional weaknesses are not a reason for assigning or perceiving added opponent strength.

Opponents may not be aware of these weaknesses.

4. Change the time available for reaching a settlement.

## Examples

Negotiators exercise patience to give opponents enough time to work out the merits of differing positions.

Negotiators spend extra effort updating their positions during recess. Strategy for subsequent meetings is adjusted.

Negotiators maintain strong commitment to original goals while enduring grinding, wearing discussions.

## Risk of Using Power

Negotiators must recognize the risk created by using power. Employing power always raises the chance that whoever is on the receiving end may react unpredictably. Furthermore, abuse through use of power leads to residual damage to the parties' relationship. The assumption that the other party lacks the courage to react to abuse is faulty. It has wrecked lots of negotiations.

## Avoiding Use of Power-Based Arguments

Negotiators should avoid using power-based arguments when trying to alter power distribution. These arguments divert attention from real issues. Diversion hurts chances for clear thinking about issues. Power-based arguments have five forms. They should not be used by negotiators.

1. Arguments of personal abuse that are irrelevant to an issue.

## Example

Suggesting a minor error in an opponent's position undermines the whole position. This consists of picking off incorrect information used in support of the opponent's position, but on which it is not dependent.

Negotiators escape the personal abuse argument. They ensure that evidence used to support their positions is relevant.

2. Arguments of absence that attempt to prove a point by asserting that it has never been disproved.

## Example

Stating that an opponent's position is untenable because its tenability is not established.

Negotiators turn aside the absence argument. They point out that the apparent absence of something neither proves nor disproves anything. The existence of an absence must actually be determined.

3. Arguments of popularity designed to discourage examination of evidence and encourage uncritical acceptance of ideas.

## Examples

"This is the general practice for this industry (popularity for)."
"It just is not done that way by anybody (popularity against)."

Negotiators blunt the popularity argument. They point out that popular support does not show decision soundness. The herd's instinct is not always right.

4. Arguments appealing to stature dispense with the need for proof while increasing deference to authority.

## Example

Introducing an expert to support or dispute the need for something.

Negotiators counter the stature argument. They provide an expert equally prestigious to refute what the first expert said. The credentials of expertise claimed by opponents should always be checked.

5. Arguments of cause and effect. These presume that if one event comes after another, the second event happened because of the first.

This is a fallacy. It should be exposed. Subsequent events are not automatically the result of preceding ones. Opponents may use this argument because of imprecise thinking.

## Example

Long ago, before people understood the use of fire in cooking, peasants in a Chinese village ate raw pork. One day during a lightening storm, a house caught fire and was destroyed. A pig was inside. It roasted. Afterward, the family who lived in the house had little left. In despair and hunger, they ate the pig. It was better than the raw pork they were used to. They shared this discovery with others. Then, regularly a house would burn down in the village. It always had a pig in it.

Negotiators also should be aware of oxymorons. An opponent might say a negotiator's position has an "unproductive solution." Or might suggest getting a "trial concession" from a negotiator to show good faith. Oxymorons should be brought to light. They are illogical phrases and therefore untenable.

## Avoiding Manipulation

Negotiators should avoid trying to manipulate opponents. It is sometimes tempting for negotiators to imagine they can discover opponents' psychological reward systems. Opponents could then be manipulated by either giving or withholding rewards. This would give negotiators an edge in power. From a practical context, manipulating someone's reward system is nonsense. First, the discovery of someone else's reward system is difficult even for trained clinicians. Second, the direction the reaction takes to reward receipt or reward deprivation varies widely. The recipient might move in the giver's wanted direction. Just as probable, they might stiffen resistance to the giver. Rewards management is a poor selection as a technique for altering the power balance in negotiations.

## Using Logic Tools

Negotiators need to consistently use logic tools to support a win-win approach.

1. *Generalization* is projecting from a particular case to a general principle, where that case truly represents that principle. This is inductive reasoning. Negotiators adept at learning as they find bits of information use this tool.

## Example

An opponent is devious on one point. It is a fair bet that they cannot be trusted too far on anything similar.

2. *Deduction* is reducing a universal situation to an individual case, where that case's characteristics embody the universal model. This is deductive reasoning. Negotiators who know that success is often a matter of proportion use this tool.

## Example

An opponent has been consistent in meeting their contractual obligations. It is a good bet they will deliver on another agreed to contract.

3. *Analogy* is transferring arguments and conflicts from subjects provoking strong feelings to like topics arousing little emotion. An opponent can look at things in a new way. This lowers the chance that high feelings will cause a negotiating failure.

## Example

An opponent is after an order-cost reduction. They also insist on the same elements as in the last contract. The negotiator suggests increasing the order size to a total that provides the cost saving wanted. Along with this, the negotiator suggests not altering the number of individual orders. The opponent views this situation as meeting their demands. The negotiator treats the several orders as one total with different dates.

4. *Syllogism* is identifying that accepting the truth for a given premise automatically produces certain conclusions. It would be inconsistent with what has already been admitted for the conclusions not to follow.

## Examples

An opponent says that terms and conditions in the negotiator's document are acceptable. The negotiator must not assume these terms and conditions represent the only ones involved. The correct conclusion is different. Opponents who omit words like "inclusive" or "all," leave the door open to introduce further terms and conditions. They do this at their convenience.

An opponent categorizes a particular point as non-negotiable. The negotiator accepts this stand. Later in the negotiation, another point is brought up similar to the non-negotiable point. By accepting the first exclusion, negotiators may involuntarily exclude other items.

The best way to deal with power questions is to combine logic tools' use with changes modifying power imbalance. This voids the need to go to other methods that produce questionable results.

The next chapter deals with influencing opponents.

# CHAPTER 11

# *INFLUENCING OPPONENTS*

*The Wolf and the Sheep*

*A Wolf, sorely wounded and bitten by dogs, lay sick and maimed in his lair. Being in want of food, he called to a Sheep who was passing, and asked him to fetch some water from a stream flowing close beside him. "For," he said, "if you will bring me drink, I will find means to provide myself with meat." "Yes," said the Sheep, "if I should bring you the drought, you would doubtless make me provide the meat also."*

Hypocritical speeches are easily seen through.
Aesop's Fables

The maximum electrical charge in the human brain is between 20 and 25 watts. The range is from original research by T. Kety, M.D. in 1948 at the University of Pennsylvania Medical School. It is certified by other researchers using measurement methods different from those Dr. Kety used. Negotiators give messages needing only the wattage required for understanding. This avoids overloading opponents. Low wattage opponents are a real problem for negotiators.

Influencing an opponent to see a negotiator's viewpoint consists of:

- gaining a high receptivity level; and
- presenting ideas effectively.

## Gaining a High Receptivity Level

Messages are effectively transferred when opponents are receptive. Receptivity is reached when opponents listen and understand. Negotiators help opponent receptivity four ways.

1. Clear static at the conscious level.
2. Use a positive talking pattern for the subconscious level.
3. Choose and use the right probes.
4. Present ideas properly.

## Clearing Static

Static impairs messages from reaching their target. Static lowers receptivity at the conscious level. To clear static, first list the types that may be met in a negotiation. Next, work on those identified as reducible. A comprehensive static list is impractical, since each negotiating situation has a different mix.

Illustrations of the differences between reducible and non-reducible static follow.

1. Reducible static is distraction from the noise of printers, telephones, and traffic; from terms used (the clearer and simpler, the better); and from climate (comfort and amenities reduce stress).
2. Non-reducible static is opponent biases, personal chemistry between the parties and non-negotiating vital concerns of opponents (involving their home life, health, or job).

Static also can be caused by boredom. This is reducible by planning longer negotiating periods first. As total time in a negotiation grows, interest lags. For example, drawing things out is often a tactic in union-management bargaining. Increasing the frequency of breaks raises attention spans. The attention span falls faster, however, in each successive period. Figure 11-1 shows this phenomena.

> **Guideline:** Negotiators must guard against boredom and loss of interest, particularly in prolonged negotiations.

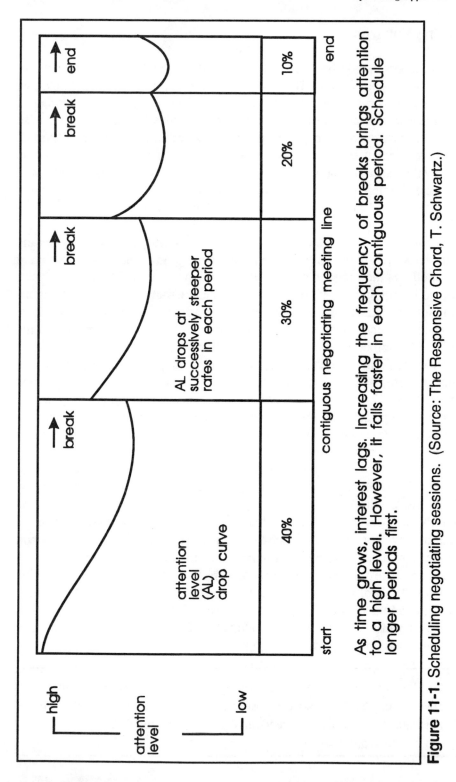

**Figure 11-1.** Scheduling negotiating sessions. (Source: The Responsive Chord, T. Schwartz.)

## Talking Patterns

How a person talks has a pattern. That pattern affects message receptivity at the subconscious level. Talking patterns consist of positive and negative elements. When positive elements dominate, listener receptivity heightens. Positive elements are questions, doubts, uncertainties, and approvals. These show that issues are open. Their benefits and arguments can be examined. Negative elements are flat assertions and contradictory emotions. These convey that issues are closed to examination. They lower listener receptivity. They are counter-productive. A classic phrase shows the effect of a negative talking pattern. "I understood what was said, but I did not like the way it was said."

Negotiators can learn their talking pattern by asking trusted colleagues and friends how they come across. Assessing responses gives negotiators a picture of the effects their talking patterns have on opponent receptivity. A precise method for finding talking pattern is to make a verbatim transcript of negotiating sessions. Each person's phrases are categorized as plus or minus. These are each divided by that person's total phrases. A talking pattern ratio is the result. This important area of communication lacks research.

There is a parallel effect of talking patterns. It happens because people store pieces of data randomly in their subconscious. These data are experiences and information. They are positive or negative. Received messages may trigger a stored data piece. The message gets a plus or minus charge. Its perception by the receiver can be changed, for instance, from a neutral or positive to a minus. This happens independently of the message's intent.

There is a third point about talking patterns. Some people are "loopers" to others. To listeners, loopers take forever to tell what they are trying to say. There are definite links between looping and culture. People in rural areas look like loopers to those from urban areas. In the U.S.A., people from the Boston-New York City-Philadelphia area think everyone else is a looper. People from other countries are often loopers to North Americans.

The opposite of looping is being abrupt. Negotiators need care when talking with people who, in their opinion, loop. The best course is to be patient. Loopers cannot change the way they talk. Trying to hurry them causes increased conflict. It is also an attack on a basic competence. The reaction is defensive and hostile.

> **Guideline:** Negotiators unsure of opponents' backgrounds, preferences, etc. should avoid discussing subjects not in the negotiation. Particularly personal preference items. They include clothing, religion, politics, and food.

## Probes

Probes are questions negotiators use to:

- start a discussion;
- keep a discussion going; and
- tie down information.

Start probes get information flowing from opponents to negotiators. They have a common characteristic. They cannot be answered by yes or no. Mastery in using start probes needs little practice. They are a common part of social communication.

Mid probes serve to keep opponents talking. Mid probes are used when opponents have given partial or insufficient information. They too, are a part of regular social communication. They need little practice to master.

Using start and mid probes aptly demands concentration.

Negotiators should use their regular conversational tone of voice. Attempting special tones, such as inquisitive or solicitous, is a waste of time. Most people cannot use contrived tones well. In trying them, negotiators risk diverting effort away from content. Listeners also may be put-off.

End probes enable negotiators to get closure or tie things together. Of the three reasons for using probes, closure is paramount. Using end probes requires considerable skill. There are two categories of end probes. In one category, negotiators put forth a problem or question. This is followed by suggesting a solution or answer. The solution or answer is stated so that the response reveals an opponent's stand. "We have a demanding timetable for this project, but it can be met. Do you agree?"

In the other category, negotiators state a sense of what an opponent seems to suggest. This is followed by asking for confirmation. The opponent response is feedback on the correctness of the negotiator's interpretation: "Your thinking appears to be that progress payments are warranted if option A is selected instead of option B."

End probes deal with more certainty than start or mid probes, and sometimes with a commitment. Their delivery is best when cushioned by an alert. This alert tells opponents an end probe is coming. It also gives the end probe rationale. The best form of alert consists of a negotiator expressing a personal need. "I would like to check my understanding at this time," followed by the end probe. Or "Could we take a minute to clear up a point for me?" followed by the end probe. Expressing a personal need takes the edge off the end probe. It removes inferring a shortcoming in an opponent's position. It avoids implied criticism that opponents are not being candid, as in "You mean to say . . ."

There are other advantages to effective probing. It helps separate first-level from second-level assumptions described in Chapter 5. It helps when reexamining assumptions made during planning. How well do they hold up in light of data uncovered during the negotiation?

## Presenting Ideas

Six actions help present ideas properly. These are idea spacing, repetition, opponent involvement, physical distance, listening, and enlarging the amount of shared information.

1. Spacing. People process information in series. The rate or speed with which they do this varies widely. It is not always associated with intelligence. There must be enough space between ideas to allow a full digestion period. Otherwise, a subsequent idea might prematurely push out the idea ahead before it is adequately digested. Alternatively, the idea following may not gain entry. Too little space is "idea tailgating." The problem for negotiators is learning the space needed between ideas for different opponents.

> **Guideline:** Leave more digestion space behind presentation of complex ideas and proposals. Leave less space for simpler ones. Learn to read an opponent's eyes. Eyes can mirror the rate and amount of comprehension.

### Example

Using examples to reenforce complex ideas helps clear away cobwebs. Well thought-out, preplanned examples are a definite plus. An example with too many parts is compound. Opponents may not be able to follow through to the original concept. This can cause wear out. Wear out leads to rejection of both the example and the idea. It is counterproductive.

> **Guideline:** Use examples that are simpler than the idea they clarify or reenforce. Avoid using compound examples - ones composed of several parts.

2. Repetition. Applied sparingly, idea repetition is useful in negotiations. Unlike saturation advertising, too much idea repetition causes throw-off. Throw-off occurs when the idea and its repetitions are purged. The opponent's mind says "Enough," and "Get out."

> **Guideline:** Limit repetitions of ideas to three times. Figure 11-2 shows a negotiation idea repetition model.

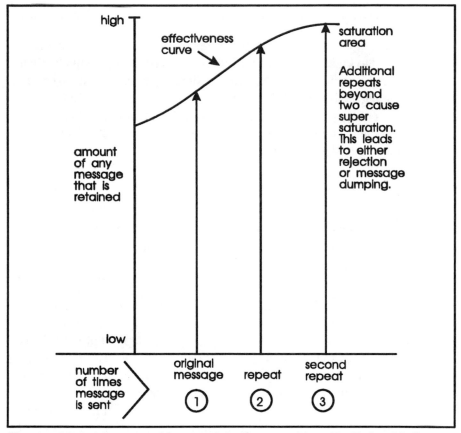

**Figure 11-2.** Idea repetition model. (Source: How To Talk with People, I. Lee.)

3. Involvement. Participation by opponents in idea development aids idea understanding. It boosts idea acceptability. Involvement is done two ways. One way is by directional thinking. This asks a question whose answer requires data use. It shows an understanding of what

the data mean. The other way explores how something would be done. By citing the steps involved, the idea is seen as workable. Proving the practicality of a proposal reduces resistance to it.

---

**Guideline:** Involve opponents in developing enactment steps when exploring the possibility of a wanted agreement. Try to do this by skipping temporarily the yes-no part of the discussion. Instead, go directly to "Let us see if this is workable, though we have not yet agreed to doing it."

---

4. Distance. In United States culture, three distances exist that negotiators need to know about. The private zone is from opponents to about two feet. Getting closer than two feet in negotiations evokes a defensive or aggressive reply. The personal zone is from two to five feet from opponents. Within that zone, physical proximity emphasizes what is said. The social zone is from five to twelve feet. That zone deemphasizes anything said.

---

**Guideline:** Make important points, statements, ideas, and confirmations that are favorable within the personal zone. Make unfavorable positions and rejections from the social zone to reduce their bite. Avoid the private zone in business negotiations.

---

5. Listening. Being a good listener has several pluses for negotiators. Superior listening skill enables them to infer, from what is said, what is important but unsaid. It enables them to hear a point of view. This is critical to evaluating merits of opponent positions. Listening helps negotiators avoid using argument-provoking replies. These often happen when initial comments are not what was hoped for or expected. Listening reduces chances for an error in timing. Timing errors cause defensive rebuttals, attempted hard lines, or too early justifications of a negotiator's positions. Listening enables negotiators to reflect upon and paraphrase opponent views. This can clarify them. It helps satisfy opponents that negotiators understand them. After that, opponents should be more attentive to the content of negotiators' statements. Opponents generally lower their defenses when discussion focuses on their side of an issue. During this time, negotiators should avoid using value statements. Negotiators should focus instead on tangible outcomes.

Listening is often poor because people receive little or no adequate listening training. People are trained in writing, reading, and speaking. But the development of their listening skills is often left to chance. Listening effectively involves hearing both what is said and what is unsaid. Negotiators improve listening skill by:

- concentrating on judging content, not delivery;
- withholding judgment until comprehension is complete;
- identifying the central theme of speakers;
- fighting distractions; and
- weighing evidence in what is said by mentally summarizing it.

Being a better listener is not as tough as it looks. People think faster than others talk. They have time to think through what is said and what it means. Practice improves the ability to stay ahead of someone taking. If a negotiator needs more time to think something over, they should say "Give me a minute to think about...."

---

**Guideline:** Fine-tune listening skills. A superb reference is Rudolph Flesch's How To Write, Speak & Think More Effectively.

---

6. Information sharing. There is always the question of who first gives solid information about issues. Many wrong ideas persist about who talks first at the start of negotiations.The prominent error is that talking first is a sign of weakness. It gives an advantage to opponents. The exact opposite is true for negotiators who plan properly. They include a starting position and ways to introduce it. Being first has two advantages. One, negotiators are saying to opponents "I trust you enough to present some information about my side." Negotiators may even say at the outset of negotiations they do not mind starting. They also should suggest that after giving some information, other information is expected back. Two, negotiators pick the information given as a starter. It should be about something negotiators think is on both parties' agendas. This does not expose a negotiator's concern with an item not on an opponent agenda. That mistake would give an opponent leverage to use when working for something wanted.

In most negotiations an issue common to both sides can be identified in preparation. Figure 11-3 shows enlarging the area of knowledge shared by negotiators and opponents. This area of shared knowledge is the Arena. It is

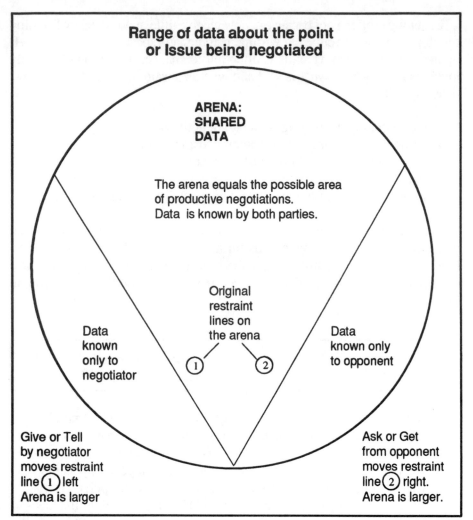

**Figure 11-3.** Enlarging the Arena. (Source: Adapted from The Johari Window, J. Hall.)

often worthwhile to restate things at the outset of a negotiation. This is one way to find out whether the Arena is now of sufficient size to do the negotiation. If it is, data outside the Arena need not divulged. It is unessential to explore more data than needed to resolve issues. When a solution is reached, negotiators must stop, though not all prepared data is used. Negotiators can evaluate the adequacy of preparation by whether they have data left over, unused. If so, preparation was adequate. This contrasts to situations where all data are used. It is not possible to know what the result might have been if more data were available.

> **Guideline:** Talking first gains some negotiating advantage and improves the relationship with opponents. Develop an economy of judgment. Know when to stop. Accept the inefficiency of over-preparation as a necessary step to getting effectiveness.

> **Guideline:** In tense situations, negotiators should be aware of when not to say anything. This is often effective in reducing tension, in " cooling" things.

## Effective Words

There are several ways to highlight what a negotiator says.

- enumerate, "The first point is..."
- emphasize, "A really important point..."
- repeat, "...nine days. Nine."
- restate, "Let us look at this another way."
- focus, "Look at this clause." [point to it]
- bridge, "We have seen the cause. Let us now look at the solution."

## Negotiations Conduct: Summary

Negotiators do better when they think about conflict as it evolves during negotiation. They avoid intimidation when armed with twin protectors, personal and organizational. Recognizing opponent need orientation lets negotiators influence opponents more. Negotiators need skill to get and keep a healthy balance in power between themselves and opponents. Logic tools are very useful. Gaining and holding opponent receptivity makes negotiators more successful.

Negotiators need three abilities to be productive.

### Task Performance

Task performance is the ability to plan and think things through analytically. It is also a mix of resolve and contention backed by the stamina to stay that way.

### Thought Process

Thought process is the ability to think clearly under pressure. This helps maintain a sense of realism. It is having common sense and judgment. These help see when to take action. It includes learning from errors and not repeating them. Judgment is a critical element for success in negotiations. People who have it, find it grows with age and experience. Those without much of it seem unable to learn it.

Critical decisions come up several times in negotiations. Negotiators must decide to act or not act [or not act prematurely]. They must balance introspection and extroversion. They must know when to press on with their conviction. For example, a negotiator failing to identify when to risk deadlock does less well after that point. No paper and pencil test exists for judgment. Therefore, people picked to negotiate should have been observed to have judgment. Unfortunately, the ability called judgment has yet to get suitable scientific investigation.

Thought process includes the ability to arrange things to see all the possibilities of what is being presented. Thinking in diagrammatical terms helps. For instance, negotiators must be able to decide whether two statements are contradictory - cannot be true together. The statements "At least some A's are B's." and "No A's are B's." might be offered as representing possible agreements. The first statement has at least four representations. A and B in overlapping circles. A and B in the same circle. A in a smaller circle within a larger B circle and vice versa. However, the second statement has only one representation. That is two independent - unconnected - circles. One A and one B. Therefore both statements could not be true together. Deciding this, negotiators avoid agreeing to something that evolves into a problem when the contradiction surfaces.

Diagrammatic thinking also helps when a negotiator needs to find exclusivity. This is whether a possibility is exclusive, exhaustive, both exclusive and exhaustive, or neither exclusive nor exhaustive. If C and D are exclusive, they do not overlap in any way, but may not cover every possibility. If they are exhaustive, they cover every possibility in the issue under review, but may not be exclusive of each another. If they are both exclusive and exhaustive, they cover every possibility but do no overlap. If they are neither exclusive nor exhaustive, they overlap and do not cover every possibility.

## Socializing [Personal Worth]

Socializing is the ability to be comfortable with others, even in stressful situations. Self-control and personal honesty combine to yield personal worth. High personal worth lets negotiators avoid being ridden by events or opponents.

Negotiators who are often successful realize that being a perfectionist reaps imperfection. Their aim is not to get everything. Instead, when reaching a genuine agreement on one issue, they move on.

The next part of this book deals with opponent styles, strategies, and tactics. It includes counteractions negotiators can take and guides for handling stylistic opponents.

# PART IV

# DEALING WITH OPPONENT STYLES, STRATEGIES AND TACTICS

One of Dr. Seuss' classic stories is about Bartholomew Cubbins. Cubbins started with one hat. Then Cubbins acquired four hundred ninety nine more. Cubbins got too many hats. That led to problems. People who negotiate may have many or just a few hats. But when they negotiate, they better be wearing the hat for negotiations. Not the hat they wear in their job as an executive or technocrat or whatever! Not the hat they wear socially! Not the hat they wear in their family! Not any other hat but the hat for negotiating.

# Dealing with Opponent Styles, Strategies, and Tactics: Introduction

Many people negotiate from a stylistic base, not an issue orientation. By recognizing opponent styles, negotiators can anticipate the actions that are part of them. Opponents usually have a primary style and at least one, sometimes two, secondary styles. Part IV examines opponent primary and secondary styles. It cites the steps negotiators consider for dealing with opponent styles.

Stylistic opponents give negotiators a competitive edge. Strategies which negate the strength of each style can be adopted. After expending a stylistic method and strategies, opponents face working the issue. Negotiator issue preparation then puts opponents at a disadvantage. Preparing around the issues is more successful than counting on style. But style is an effective support to issue orientation. That is its rightful use.

There are various ways to look at style. The approach used here is based on Carl Jung's personality model. It is practical. It is easy to understand. Jung was a Swiss psychiatrist. Although a contemporary and friend of Sigmund Freud, Jung differed with Freud. Jung emphasized drives that direct people's actions instead of emphasizing their past sexual development. Jung is not first in saying behavior comes from four drives. The Greek philosopher-physician, Hippocrates, used four "humors" as the basis for behavior. Unfortunately, Hippocrates used bodily fluids, such as phlegm. Meyers Briggs use four indicators - fast track, catalyst, hard charger and power broker. Jung, Meyers Briggs and a lot of lesser lights owe much of their notoriety to Hippocrates.

Jung's model is altered to fit the subject of stylistic opponents. This revised model is a convenience for negotiators. The tactics generally used in, but not exclusive to, each style are discussed. Methods for effectively dealing with each style accompany its description.

# CHAPTER 12

# *OPPONENT STYLES*

### The Three Tradesmen

*A Great City was besieged, and its inhabitants were called together to consider the best means of protecting it from the enemy. A Bricklayer earnestly recommended bricks as affording the best material for an effective resistance. A Carpenter, with equal enthusiasm, proposed timber as a preferable method of defense. Upon which a Currier stood up and said, "Sirs, I differ from you altogether; there is no material equal to a covering of hides; and nothing so good as leather."*

Every man for himself.
Aesop's Fables

## The Four Opponent Styles

Non-issue oriented opponents use four primary styles. Each style is the result of two drivers that are part of Jung's model. Each driver has a dominant belief.

1. Control is the drive to dominate and rule others. Its main belief is in the correctness of direct, unbridled rivalry.
2. Disregard is the drive to discount others. Its main belief is that passive endurance and extreme attention to detail are most important.
3. Deference is the drive to let others take the lead. Its main belief is that disinterest or patience have the most value.
4. Trust is the drive to include others as working partners. Its main belief is that collaboration is best.

Figure 12-1 shows how these drivers blend to produce the four stylistic opponents. The styles and assumptions underlying each are described next.

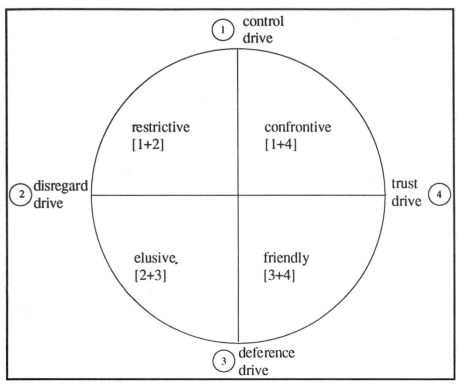

**Figure 12-1.** Opponent styles. (Source: Work of C. Jung.)

1. *Restrictive.* Control combines with disregard to assume that negotiators must be forced to settle. They automatically are uncooperative. This is the way things are. These opponents expect people to act in their own interest in whatever way necessary. Restrictive style opponents want only win or deadlock outcomes.
2. *Elusive.* Disregard combines with deference to assume that negotiators must be avoided or kept remote. They represent a source of trouble. They will do what they feel like doing. The perception is that people cannot influence other's. No matter how they act. It is useless to deal on a personal level. It is best to focus on procedures and rules. Elusive style opponents urgently want to survive negotiation. Staying unchanged is next in importance. Getting results is tertiary.
3. *Friendly.* Deference and trust combine to assume that negotiators are

usually cooperative, even sympathetic. A sense of fair play is a main influence. There are, of course, competitive situations. By taking a larger view while avoiding detail and nitpicking, things can be sketched out. Friendly style opponents covet keeping relationships with negotiators. This is irrespective of whether anything of substance is done.

4. *Confrontive.* Trust and control combine to assume that negotiators seek fairness. They appreciate the need to contest issues while working with others to get a solid agreement. The view is that collaboration is preferable to obstruction. People seek objectivity if they are not treated subjectively. Confrontive style opponents seek the best total agreement practicable. The agreement should be heavily backed by merit and mutual commitment to its enactment.

Figure 12-2 shows how these styles relate to the need orientations described in Chapter 9.

## Style Similarities

Restrictive and confrontive styles are initiators. Elusive and friendly styles are mostly reactive.

Restrictive and confrontive style opponents get high numbers of settlements. However, commitment to agreements with restrictive style opponents is less than to confrontive ones. This is because the tactics used by restrictive style opponents leave a bad taste with the other party. This is true even when the agreement is fair. Bad taste converts to active hostility in agreements lopsided toward restrictive style opponents. Such agreements have a good chance of unraveling. They may abort totally. Restrictive style opponent's tactics use strategies of force and intimidation. Commitment to agreements with confrontive style opponents usually are firm. They hold up longest. They have the best chances for completion.

Elusive and friendly style opponents are less productive than the other two styles. This is because they fix on things other than getting agreements. Survival is the focus for elusive style opponents. Relationship maintenance is the focus for friendly style opponents. Commitment to agreements with elusive style opponents is especially tenuous. Negotiating with an elusive style opponent is boring and taxing. It is an unrewarding experience. It is like being run over by a flock of stampeding sheep. It takes forever. Social aspects, not issue merit, dominate commitment to agreements with friendly style opponents. At times that may be enough. It is still less desirable than settlements hammered out through contention and examination.

Each style has an optimum application.  The applications differ.

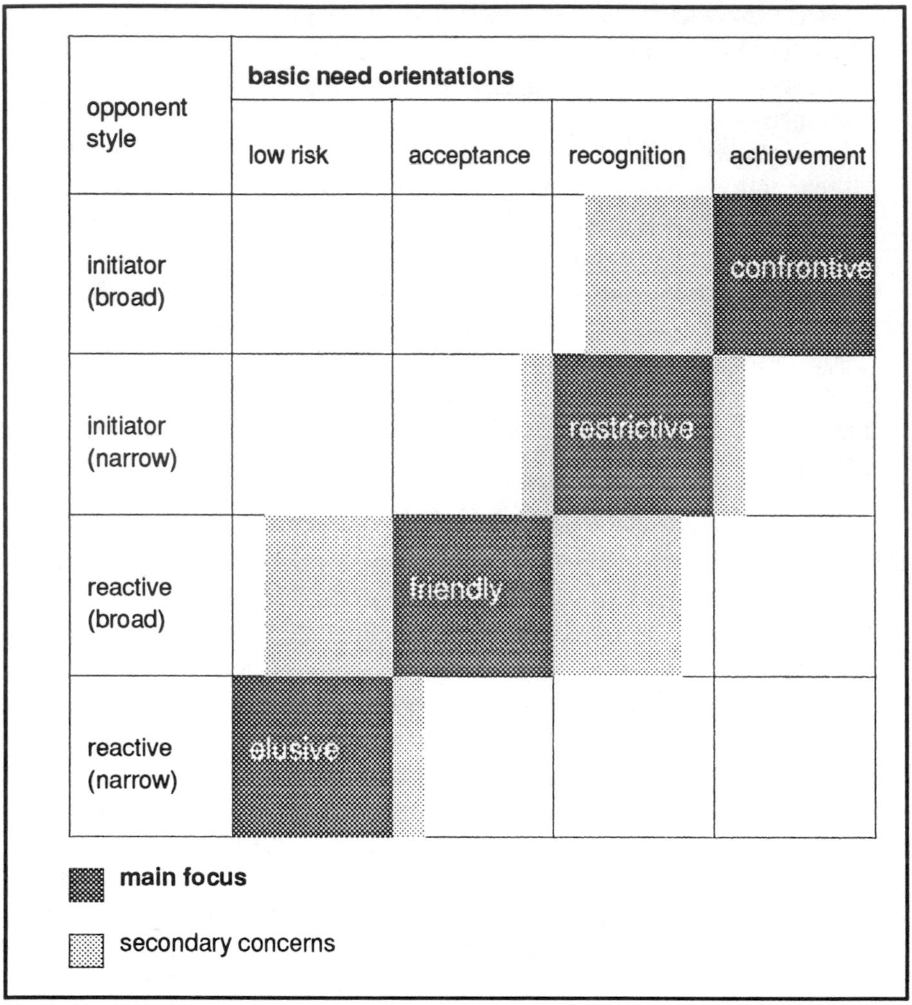

| opponent style | basic need orientations | | | |
|---|---|---|---|---|
| | low risk | acceptance | recognition | achievement |
| initiator (broad) | | | | confrontive |
| initiator (narrow) | | | restrictive | |
| reactive (broad) | | friendly | | |
| reactive (narrow) | elusive | | | |

■ **main focus**

▨ secondary concerns

**Figure 12-2.** Opponent styles matched with need orientation. (Source: Works of A. Maslow and C. Jung.)

A restrictive style may be sensible when the issue is a "must settle," involves high stakes and a terminal conflict.  Restrictive style can be a last resort.  After other styles fail to produce a needed agreement.

An elusive style has merit when the issue is routine or has heavy detail demanding painstaking review.  Elusive may be okay when other factors, such as conforming to policy, are ahead of the need for settlement.  An elusive style can be used to intentionally delay agreement.

A friendly style is applicable when the issue requires exuberance, enthusiasm, diplomacy, and tact. Two examples are smoothing ruffled feelings or where detail is not critical. Friendly style is a good approach for people where the issue is poor performance by their side. It reduces the urge by the other side to punish the poor performance.

A confrontation style is best when the issue is a "must settle," involves high stakes and a contentious conflict. Confrontive style helps long term relations.

## Need For Flexibility

Different optimal applications for the four styles increase the need for negotiator flexibility. On the one hand, it is important to let opponents use the styles they want. Concurrently, negotiators must act complementary to each issue. By doing so, opponents must work harder to keep up. They cannot use a strategy based on the predictability of negotiator styles. A consistent negotiating style is as harmful as is an inconsistent management style.

Negotiators know that categorizing an opponent's style is very helpful. But, over reliance on categorization is risky. People do not often fit neatly into categories, though they may rely heavily on stylism when negotiating.

The next chapter discusses stylistic based tactics, counters to them, and options for handling stylistic opponents.

# CHAPTER 13

# *STYLISTIC-BASED TACTICS AND COUNTERS*

*The Ass and His Shadow*

*A Traveler hired an Ass to convey him to a distant place. The day being intensely hot, and the sun shining in its strength, the Traveler stopped to rest, and sought shelter from the heat under the Shadow of the Ass. As this afforded the only protection for one, and as the Traveler and the owner of the Ass both claimed it, a violent dispute arose between them as to which of them had the right to the Shadow. The Traveler asserted that he had, with the hire of the Ass, hired his Shadow also. The quarrel proceeded from words to blows, and while the men fought, the Ass galloped off.*

In quarreling about the shadow we often lose the substance.
Aesop's Fables

## Stylistic-Based Tactics

Tactics are the actions for enacting strategy. Each opponent style uses tactics based on assumptions about negotiators. Different styles use some of the same tactics. Each tactic appears in many forms. Only the central tactic is described here.

## Restrictive Style Opponent Tactics

Coercion, fear, and threat characterize the tactics used by restrictive style opponents.

## Tactic.

*Deputy.* A restrictive style opponent claims limited authority. This is an attempt to keep negotiator demands to a low level. Opponents also use this tactic to simulate the need to refer to higher authority. They seek time to learn and evaluate negotiator positions without revealing much of theirs.

## Examples

"The legal department will tie us up forever if you want all these terms put in the formal contract. Trust me."

"Our finances are in rotten shape. We cannot buy much. If we buy anything, we need special, extended terms."

## Counter.

Deputies are a fact in some negotiations, a sham in others. The outset of the negotiation is the best place to minimize the effect of this tactic. Negotiators inform opponents that they will tell their authority limits - in as much detail as policy permits. Negotiators then expect opponents to do the same. If an opponent agrees, the negotiator proceeds. If not, the indication is the opponent will use the deputy tactic.

Negotiators should write down authority claimed by opponents. Opponents seeing this, experience a sobering thought. They cannot later claim a different authority level.

## Tactic.

*Diminish.* A restrictive style opponent with a weaker position compared to a negotiator's tries to gain parity. They apply negative, but unrelated, descriptions to a negotiator's position. This false characterization is to reduce the negotiator's positional strength.

## Examples

"You have no right to complain about my performance. All you big companies are bloated with extra people. Try doing the job we little guys have to do. You make mistakes too."

"Your engineers said we could deliver late because your schedulers were mixed up. Your sales people changed shipping dates for two of your big customers."

"Your approach is unheard of, too radical."

## Counter.

Diminution invokes the argument that unpopular things are automatically not good. The counter is to let opponents work through this gambit, then insist on returning to the issue's merits. Argument about the validity of the trumped-up negative uses time poorly. It only serves to deplete a negotiator's energies.

## Tactic.

*Irrevocable.* Restrictive style opponents try to go around negotiators to other, probably higher, organization levels. They present the negotiators with statements like "The Vice President said we should get your signature and go forward on this" or "Your operating people want this now, so let's get the paperwork out of the way." This tactic is to intimidate the negotiator. It tries to by-pass examining the issue.

## Counter.

Irrevocable is an appeal to higher authority. It is handled two ways, hinging on the negotiator's organization's protocol. Negotiators can refuse to go forward. Opponents are told to recontact the other person(s) and get written authorization backing up opponent claims. Alternatively, opponents can be put in limbo while negotiators check with the other person(s). This should be done carefully. It risks that negotiators and the other person(s) might get into unneeded conflict. That can be an opponent's goal.

If the opponent's claim is true, a negotiator better get their duties defined. More opponents might discover they can be by-passed easily.

## Tactic.

*Startle.* Restrictive style opponents take action without informing negotiators. Perhaps they invite competitors to the negotiation. They might move the physical site in the midst of the discussion. The purpose of startle is to destabilize negotiator thinking. To divert it from the issue.

## Examples

"This is our lawyer who will sit in on our meeting. Just happened to be here and is interested in this deal."

"We know delivery is critical. We cannot meet it without overtime. That raises the price 23%. We will make up the extra cost to you later. On another contract."

## Counter.

Startles cannot be avoided. The counter, however, should be to make the startle cost opponents something. The easiest and most readable cost is delay. In effect it says to opponents, "Every time you pull a startle, it will lengthen the negotiation." This cost is also borne by negotiators. It is, however, a better way than arguing about the startle or saying it is unjustified. Arguing here uses negotiator energies for a non-issue. Depleting negotiator energy might be a purpose behind the tactic. The delay offers negotiators time to assess the startle. To intelligently plot a course of action.

Negotiators should not automatically assume evil motives when a startle occurs. They should ponder the facts and background before making a judgment. Is this an intentional tactic or is it unintentional?

The four tactics above are not poor because they may be morally questionable. They are poor because they do not contribute to settlement. They are less effective because they do not add longevity to outcomes. Restrictive style opponents do use a beneficial tactic. Like most effective tactics, this has no counter. If it works, its use cannot be proved by the others.

## Tactic.

*Reunion.* Restrictive style opponents sometimes know where negotiators stand on an issue. They then take a plausible position somewhat away from that stand. Actually, the negotiators' position is okay with the opponents. Opponents let negotiators move them back to the original position. This looks like a concession to negotiators.

Restrictive style opponents get two advantages from a reunion that works. They are where they wanted to be by accepting through negotiation a position already acceptable. They have seemingly made a concession. Now negotiators owe the restrictive style opponents a concession, quid pro quo.

## Example

The president of a company knew that a principal customer group was holding an important industry coordinating meeting. The president discovered one decision ahead of any formal announcement. The group had decided to insist on higher quality standards from suppliers. The president instructed marketing and engineering executives to develop costs on these unpublished, new standards. The data showed the standards were well within the company's current capability. The new standards would even benefit the company's products by improving their performance. The president immediately announced a product improvement program in personal letters to high level customer executives. The program exceeded the new industry standards. The customer executives deduced that the standards the supplier described signified a substantial price increase. Customer group representatives convinced the supplier to lower its announced product goals to the new industry specifications. They now became more supportive for placing orders at this company. It had not upset their industry group plans. A material increase in the supplier's sales took place. It was attributable to the supplier president's reunion strategy.

## Restrictive Style Opponent Behavior

Restrictive style opponents strive for any advantage possible. They interpret things in ways that put them in a favorable light. Restrictive style opponents talk much. They listen little. They use facts to get a surrender. They adopt fixed positions while bulldozing ahead over others. Restrictive style opponents are hard working, aggressive, and opinionated. Their interest mostly is in negotiations that raise their esteem and help personal progress. What restrictive style opponents have not learned is that success does not always come from succeeding. There are specific steps negotiators must take in dealing with restrictive style opponents.

1. Let them vent negative emotions. This is their standard opening approach.
2. Do not argue directly. This increases their combative bent. It confirms their feeling that a negotiator is an enemy to be vanquished.
3. Probe flat assertions or easy yeses. Distinguish between phrases of comprehension versus agreement. This also checks progress and tacks things down as negotiations move along.
4. Use facts and provide details. Restrictive styles respond to these.

They value hard information.
5. Be firm and show resolve. They do not accept equivocation. Any sign of weakness heightens their hunger for a kill.
6. Emphasize the benefits from negotiator proposals that appeal to their need orientations of greed and pride.

## Elusive Style Opponent Tactics

Tactics used by elusive style opponents focus on avoidance. Delay and procrastination characterize them.

### Tactic.

*Retire.* Elusive style opponents give the impression of backing away or being in subordinate positions. This is to lull negotiators into overconfidence. Then elusive style opponents start at the beginning as though no progress was made. Time, effort, and energy are expended fruitlessly.

### Example

"I find our two hour negotiation valuable. As a starting point. But, back here on page one is a split infinitive. Experience shows that clerical errors indicate other, and serious, problems may exist. We need to carefully review all."

### Counter.

The counter to retire is not to let it happen. Negotiators should summarize at appropriate times as progress is made. Elusive style opponents may not agree that something is settled. They can be confronted with the need to agree or disagree that it has been explored adequately. This ties-off that a part of the discussion is completed, before going on to the next part. It avoids or at least reduces the exasperating rehashing on which elusive style opponents thrive.

### Tactic.

*Specimen.* Elusive style opponents often give selective data quantitatively arranged. They assume that others will accept it as accurately representing the total of things. This includes the use of quasi-quantified data, pictorial representations instead of graphs, percentages instead of actual numbers, etc. Elusive style opponents may also give excessive detail from which the specimen was drawn. This is an attempt to hide the absence of specific data in sufficient quantity.

## Examples

"We used a statistical model, including an f test." Since there are two f tests, a negotiator needs to know which was used to find if it was the correct one.

"The average salary paid our people is higher than the market for similar jobs." There are three averages, mean, mode and median. Without knowing which was used, a negotiator cannot tell if the average is correct in the context used.

## Counter.

The counter to specimen is to express interest in the back-up information. It should be evaluated by the negotiator - "Is it truly represented by the specimen?" Technical knowledge may be required, especially where statistical methods are used. Valid statistical methods can be used for the wrong application to get a desired answer.

## Tactic.

*Virtue.* Elusive style opponents sometimes are in an obvious weak position vis-a-vis negotiators. They assign qualities to their position in an attempt to gain parity. They hope to achieve a halo effect. Virtue is the opposite of diminish. It has a better chance of succeeding because it uses positive expressions.

## Example

"Actually, the load of parts we failed to deliver turned out bad. They were beyond the acceptable failure limit. You are better off. Your assembly using those parts would have been rejected."

"No one in our business meets safety specifications. They are just to keep the regulators happy. Gives them something to do."

## Counter.

Virtue is best countered by forbearance or, if fitting, humor. Putting a weaker case in a better wrapper does not change its value. Negotiators must insist on returning to the facts.

Many elusive style opponent tactics cause negotiators deep frustration. These tactics needlessly draw out resolution time without adding to quality.

Elusive style opponents do use a tactic that can be beneficial. Though identifiable, there is no counter to it.

## Tactic.

Equanimity. Sometimes anger or impetuous behavior seems justified, like when a person's honesty is attacked. The greater benefit may be in withholding overt reaction. Patience may be misjudged as indecision. However, it provides elusive style opponents time to reflect and measure their response with less emotional influence. Acquiring equanimity often comes from experience. Its users show self-governance. They are less impulsive.

### Elusive Style Opponent Behavior

Elusive style opponents seek to survive through opting for perfection. They repress from conscious thought anything repugnant to themselves. They are superficial. They talk little and listen little. They are most comfortable in neutral gear. Elusive style opponents have not learned that negotiation is not entirely a numbers activity. Often, elusive style opponents are plodders, loners, moody, and work by the book. What looks like meekness is compensated for by being intense. Negotiations that most interest elusive style opponents are routine. Those with a known expectation. Negotiators can take specific steps that help deal with elusive style opponents.

1. Behave reassuringly, move ahead slowly. This establishes trust. It recognizes the elusive style's innate reticence and suspicion.
2. Do not talk too much or too long. This reduces opportunity for elusive styles to mentally bail out.
3. Use lots of detail while keeping elusive styles involved in exploring its meaning. They like to get into all the corners.
4. Avoid exploiting their passiveness. Their behavior might alter radically.
5. Guide the forward progress constantly. Elusive style opponents seldom initiate forward movement.
6. Emphasize the benefits that appeal to their single consuming need orientation - the absence of risk. This is security.

## Friendly Style Opponent Tactics

Friendly style opponents use tactics that emphasize a few small goals, easy achievement and amicability.

## Tactic.

*Crisscross.* This tactic has two dimensions. First, one issue is randomly subdivided. It is presented as several disconnected, nonadjacent issues. Negotiators must pull the issue together and get friendly style opponents to accept its integrity. Second, several superficial issues are offered that should not be on the agenda. This attempts to disguise the few issues important to friendly style opponents.

## Examples

"Let us try to look at this overall. The issues are really related and the broad view is best. We can sort out details later." This is okay if the issues are not separate. But, they usually are.

"Too much time on these things over complicates deals."

## Counter.

The element of randomness makes crisscross hard to deal with. Negotiators must sort through the muck to find the pearl. Patience coupled with constant, evenly applied pressure to move ahead, is the best counter to crisscross. The need for progress is the rationale for recomposing fragmented issues. For scrubbing junk cargo. For sticking to priorities.

## Tactic.

*Ganging.* Friendly style opponents often try to enlist the aid of others, even negotiators, to make their cases. The others may not even be involved in the negotiation. This action is based on the false premise that everyone is as empathetic as they.

## Examples

"My brother-in-law on the West Coast is pretty sharp, even though he is not in this business. He says we should..."

"This magazine article, although on a different subject, illustrates my point about how economics impacts this situation."

## Counter.

Ganging, like crisscross, has an element of randomness. That causes difficulty. It seldom brings relevant analysis to bear on issues. Questioning the relevance of someone's opinion draws negotiators off the real question. The better counter to ganging is forbearance. Negotiators reject irrelevancies by simply ignoring them. Negotiators can finesse ganging by saying "That source is usually good, but this is a special case."

## Tactic.

*Synthetic limits.* Placing synthetic limits on what can be done is doubly attractive to friendly style opponents. First, it shows more progress than is made. Progress is measured against a smaller total constrained by the synthetic limits. Second, it downplays any risk that might emerge from the creative problem-solving needed for complex issues. That process has too much effort.

## Example

"Rome was not built in a day."

## Counter.

Synthetic limits are expressed in the same terms as real ones - money, time, space, authority, etc. Negotiators should, as a rule, probe all limits expressed by opponents. Those that look unverified need to be challenged. The challenge might be in asking for confirmation of the source for the limits. For friendly style opponents, polite skepticism or patience is usually enough of a reaction. Negotiators should then push ahead as though the synthetic limits were not put forth.

## Friendly Style Opponent Behavior

Friendly style opponents also make ample use of reunion. They took at the positive side of something. They talk much. They listen only partially. Friendly style opponents meander and will not stick to points. They often interject unrelated social issues into negotiations. They are the least competitive of the four styles.

Typically, friendly style opponents are charming, cajolers and attractive personalities. Negotiation matters involving talking versus doing are of most interest. The "big picture" viewpoint predominates. Friendly style opponents fear harming a relationship more than seeking the joy of completing a negotiation successfully. There are specific actions that help deal with friendly style opponents.

1. Keep them on track, yet give room to wander. They lack self-discipline. Avoid introducing distractions. Enough will occur naturally.
2. Uncover unspoken disagreements and probe easy yeses.
   Friendly styles avoid being candid in an attempt not to hurt anyone's feelings. Their actual position must be found and dealt with, but gently.
3. Avoid inundating them with facts. They combine the written with the verbal. A tune out happens if too much data overload their circuit.
4. Avoid exploiting their good fellowship. A friendly style's behavior might alter radically.
5. Guide the forward progress constantly. They accept moderate direction.
6. Emphasize the benefits that appeal to their need orientations of pride, interdependence and safety.

## Confrontive Style Opponent Tactics

Confrontive style opponents use tactics that combine collaboration and confrontation. These emphasize negotiator involvement.

## Tactic.

*Real limits.* Confrontive style opponents seek to define and set mutually recognizable limits that exist for both parties. The purpose is moving negotiations along while blocking out unnecessary items. This tactic can benefit well prepared negotiators. Negotiators must exercise care not to be put into a position of excluding items they want on the agenda.

## Example

> "We are committed to a schedule that gets this deal done today or passes it for other opportunities. That means getting the details on the main points done. We are willing to work all day. But at six PM we need to tell our management that we have a deal. Is this possible from your side?"

## Counter.

Check the rationale. Does it make sense. Test any limits that do not.

Other tactics used most often by confrontive style opponents - equanimity, reunion, and virtue - have been described.

## Confrontive Style Opponent Behavior

Confrontive style opponents are very competitive. They have the endurance and exuberance of ideas to keep at it. They state positions clearly. They listen well. While confrontive style opponents are driving and aggressive, they are also supportive of others. They consider trying new approaches. Negotiations having risks, innovations, and challenges to creativity are of most interest. They believe agreements are possible where both sides share in winning, but not necessarily equally. What confrontive style opponents have not learned is that a person's best skills can sometimes become great handicaps. There are specific actions negotiators should take when dealing with a confrontive style opponent.

1. Anticipate any weaknesses in negotiator data. Be ready to do something about weaknesses. Confrontive style opponents are methodical enough to uncover most weaknesses in other's positions.
2. Check continually their understanding. Monitor the pace, Confrontive styles move along quickly and might carry negotiators into unwanted areas.
3. Use quantity of data where available. Confrontive styles respond to this.
4. Avoid overstating or being imprecise about benefits. Any hint of a falsehood will be met with an attack.
5. Prove the use of preparation and planning. Confrontive styles respect and respond favorably to these.
6. Emphasize benefits that appeal to their need orientations of pride, greed and interdependence.

Figure 13-1 ties opponent style tactics to their primary argument appeal (see "Primary Argument Appeal," Chapter 10).

## Guidelines for Dealing with All Opponents

Negotiators should hold to four guidelines when working with opponents. These apply whatever the opponent style.

|  | Primary Argument Appeal | | | |
|---|---|---|---|---|
| **Tactic and Style Often Using It** | Personal Abuse | Absence of Proof | Popularity | Stature-Imposing Source or Mode |
| Deputy [RSO] |  | ✓ |  |  |
| Diminish [RSO] |  |  | ✓ |  |
| Irrevocable [RSO] | ✓ |  |  |  |
| Startle [RSO] | ✓ |  |  |  |
| Retire [ESO] |  | ✓ |  |  |
| Specimen [ESO] |  |  |  | ✓ |
| Virtue [ESO/CSO] |  |  | ✓ |  |
| Crisscross [FSO] |  |  |  | ✓ |
| Ganging [FSO] |  |  | ✓ |  |
| Synthetic Limits [FSO] |  |  |  | ✓ |

Tactics not appealing to a primary argument and style often using them:

| Reunion | RSO / FSO / CSO |
|---|---|
| Equanimity | ESO / CSO |
| Real Limits | CSO |

**Figure 13-1.** Tactics related to primary argument appeal. (Source: Sparks Consultants.)

1. Let opponents behave naturally. Do not try to manipulate opponent behavior. Instead, adjust as much as possible to complement the opponent style. Do not add stress to the negotiation. Stress impairs good judgment.
2. Use the opponent's value system to increase receptivity. Remember Ben Franklin's way. Speak of benefits to the opponent interest rather than the logic of why a proposal is valuable. The benefits must be put in an acceptable context. They must agree with the direction in which an opponent leans. This is either benefits now or benefits later plus the interest dominating their attention - power or pride or greed or continuance.
3. Guide opponents to conclusions wanted. Let them say them. The realization of them. This sets the approval level higher than it would be

otherwise. However, this is the hardest guideline. Whether an opponent can draw the conclusion is not always obvious. If they cannot, much time is spent for no useful purpose.

4. Avoid the animal urge to dominate a seemingly weak opponent. Weakness can be feigned. Reticence can be mistaken for weakness. Style, like any behavior, can swing quickly. A tiger can be let out. The negotiation can get needlessly complex.

The next chapter explores secondary styles and some influences of culture on style.

# CHAPTER 14

# *STYLE MOVEMENT*

### The Cat and Venus

*A Cat fell in love with a handsome young man, and entreated Venus to change her into the form of a woman. Venus consented to her request and transformed her into a beautiful damsel, so that the youth saw her and loved her, and took her home as his bride. While the two were reclining in their chamber, Venus wishing to discover if the Cat in her change of shape had also altered her habits of life, let down a mouse in the middle of the room. The Cat, quite forgetting her present condition, started from the couch and pursued the mouse, wishing to eat it. Venus was much disappointed and again caused her to return to her former shape.*

Nature exceeds nurture.
Aesop's Fables

## Secondary Styles

Opponents may not stay with their primary style throughout a negotiation. They will return to it several times. Style change comes from three causes - natural, directive, and reactive.

### Natural

Natural cause is like water flowing down its handy trench. An opponent's experience and personal makeup combine to shift style. The action is subconscious. The movement is toward less trust. Negotiators must avoid actions

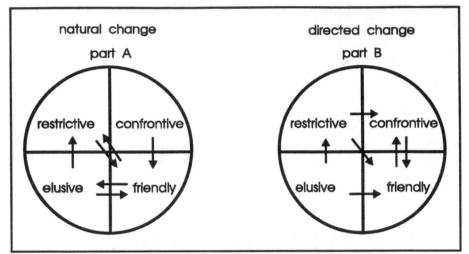

**Figure 14-1.** Secondary style. (Source: Work of C. Jung.)

that start this movement. Reducing an opponent's trust makes negotiation harder. When natural cause alters opponent style, skill coupled with patience is needed to modify the secondary style. Part A of Figure 14-1 shows style change due to natural cause.

## Directive

Directive cause is like purposely altering the flow of water. An opponent alters primary style. The reason may be expediency. Or a try at a complementary style with a negotiator. The action is planned. It is conscious. Directive cause is choice. It can be influenced. This change is shown in Part B of Figure 14-1. Very seldom does anyone purposely adopt the elusive style. It is too tedious and unrewarding for most people.

## Reactive

Reactive cause results from two actions. A negotiator blocks an opponent from reaching an important goal. The opponent bounces off the block to a decision point having three options.

1. Attack the block in an attempt to breach it and reach the original goal.
2. Retreat to a deadlock or abort the negotiation; go elsewhere.
3. Seek an alternative goal or a modification of the original goal that offers a better chance of agreement.

Next, a negotiator pushes forward before an opponent has time to pick from the options above. This shows poor judgment or a lack of discipline by a negotiator. Crowding opponents this way is a mistake. The general reaction is to select either option one - attack, or two - abort. Pushing opponents at the wrong time bans the third option. This option is most favorable for negotiators. Figure 14-2 shows the reactive cause. Reactive cause can usually be influenced since opponents select it.

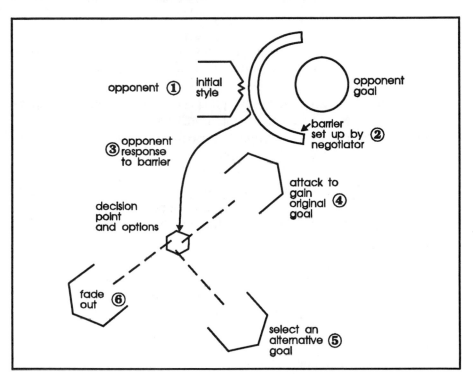

**Figure 14-2.** Reactive change. (Source: Flights, Games and Debates, A. Rapoport.)

---

**Guideline:** The briefer the negotiation time, the less likely significant style shifts take place to compound a negotiator's work.

---

**Guideline:** In any negotiation, opponents will evidence at least one secondary style attributable to cause. Negotiators should remember this action when planning future negotiations with the same opponents.

## Cultural Influences on Styles

Many techniques discussed apply to negotiating with people from other cultures. Culture is how people develop mental and moral positions. It stems from education and adoption of behavior ascribed to a class or group one belongs to or wants to join. People can be a mix of several cultures. One will dominate.

There are six important areas for analysis when negotiating with other cultures besides the issues.

1. *Sensitivity*. What is opponent expectation regarding rank, age and protocol? Answers to these questions avoid annoying opponents unnecessarily.
2. *Authority*. How much routine and precedence has an opponent emphasized as needed to govern the negotiation? The answer to this question reveals opponent authority. The narrower the authority, the more dependency on structure. The narrower the authority, the more often opponents need to consult with others.
3. *Rivalries*. How much internecine arguing is there within the opponent organization? The more rivalry, the more opponent negotiators must avoid getting caught in the middle. Internal rival factions will join to attack outsiders.
4. *Opponent support*. What circumstances are evident about support from the opponent organization? Do major slip-ups occur often? Is carelessness obvious? Answers to these questions point the way to the reason for seemingly uncalled for cancellations and postponements.
5. *Personalties*. Does an opponent make it especially difficult to cultivate personal relations? This is usually a sign of heavy reliance on structure. Position and rank are more important than individual character. Trust developed in this climate centers on job positions or organizations, not on individuals.
6. *Details*. What is opponent emphasis regarding detail in the final agreement? How does the emphasis on agreement detail or lack of it compare with the emphasis on details in guarantees? Is the emphasis greater, equal, or less? To illustrate, an opponent seeks substantial detail in the final agreement. If this opponent seeks the same detail in guarantees, such as warranties, the approach is consistent. However, suppose this opponent wants to keep guarantees general. Then, negotiators can conclude that this opponent will make liberal interpretations about warranties, etc.

## Two Languages

Some people see an agreement as real, as compared to alien, when it is in their own language. This is especially true cross-culturally. Putting agreements in both languages helps avoid interpretation difficulties later. It strengthens the agreement because of its complimentary effect on the other party. Dual language clearly shows recognition of and respect for the other party. It conveys acceptance as an equal. Simultaneously, it must be clear which language governs the agreement. Translation may alter intent. Figure 14-3 broadly compares negotiating styles based on different cultures.

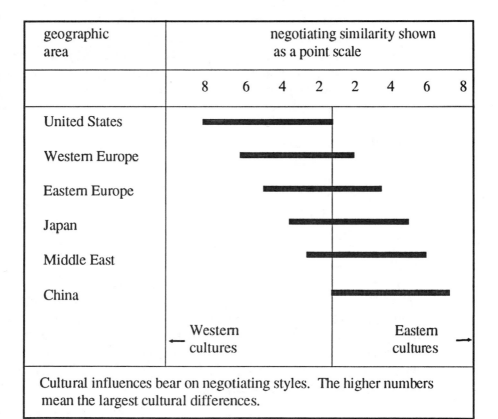

| geographic area | negotiating similarity shown as a point scale | | | | | | | |
|---|---|---|---|---|---|---|---|---|
| | 8 | 6 | 4 | 2 | 2 | 4 | 6 | 8 |
| United States | | | | | | | | |
| Western Europe | | | | | | | | |
| Eastern Europe | | | | | | | | |
| Japan | | | | | | | | |
| Middle East | | | | | | | | |
| China | | | | | | | | |

← Western cultures                    Eastern cultures →

Cultural influences bear on negotiating styles. The higher numbers mean the largest cultural differences.

**Figure 14-3.** Cultural override on negotiating styles. (Source: Sparks Consultants.)

## Two Ways To Look At Things

Some examples of culture's impact is how North Americans broadly look at values, organization and career growth compared to Mainland Chinese.

|                | **North American**                        | **Mainland Chinese**                             |
| -------------- | ----------------------------------------- | ------------------------------------------------ |
| Values         | individualism                             | team work                                        |
|                | incentive driven                          | accomplishment driven                            |
|                | respect intellectual property rights      | little respect for intellectual property rights  |
|                | loyalty not a top priority                | loyalty very important                           |
| Organization   | big companies                             | small, family owned                              |
|                | established systems                       | loosely structured                               |
|                | hard to change                            | flexible                                         |
|                | career development very important         | little career development                        |
|                | technical people far from markets         | technical people close to markets                |
| Career growth  | structured                                | on one's own                                     |
|                | planned                                   | decided by owners                                |
|                | step by step                              | very fast track                                  |

Some other cultural differences to be aware of are:

- uncertainty - some cultures cherish security and career stability while other reward risk takers;
- gender - in masculine cultures, money and things equal great concern, while in female cultures, people and environments are regarded highly;
- individual-collective - in some cultures success is defined by individual performance while in others, group membership and acceptance define success; and
- dynamicism - some cultures focus on long term orientations of thrift and perseverance while others emphasize the near term.

## Examples of cultural based things to watch out for in different countries:

England - steer clear of gossip about royalty, politics and religion; call people from Scotland, Scottish, not Scots.

Italy - steer clear of politics; okay to talk about business, local news and family matters; if invited to a home, take wine or chocolates or flowers [odd numbers only].

Japan - never ask questions host cannot answer; small gifts are always okay, wrap in rice paper, but not in white [means death].

Taiwan - take gifts, present with both hands; do not overdo compliments; do not express too much admiration for something - you may get it as a gift.

Germany - do not hard sell; be on time and sophisticated; show a real knowledge of their music, theater and literature.

Saudi Arabia - expect to see others in the room, private appointments are rare; family comes before business, so do moslems over infidels [non-believers]; don't give handkerchief as a gift - it means breaking a relationship.

Asia - do not offer a tip, bad manners [if needed, present gratuity in sealed envelope, which is seen as a gift].

Mexico and Brazil - spend time talking about family, it is an ice breaker; gifts are okay.

Australia - expect to join in heated discussions, they welcome that; don't offer unsolicited advice [hurts their pride].

South Korea - avoid four of anything, four is considered bad luck; the longer a person bows at the end of something, the more pleasure they got.

## Sources of data about other countries and cultures.

The best is the chatty CULTURGRAMS published by Brigham Young University. These are for about 100 countries. Each 4 page report covers customs, courtesies, people, lifestyle, country and a map. Practical tips are emphasized. The pamphlets are inexpensive. They are bought separately, in groups or in complete sets. They are reissued every 2 years. SOURCE: David M. Kennedy Center for International Studies, Publications Services, 280 HRCB, Brigham Young University, Provo, Utah 84602. 1-801-378-6528.

The next best is the terse BACKGROUND NOTES from the U.S.A. State Department. These are for about 200 countries. Each 6 to 10 page report covers geography, people, history, government, political condition, economy, foreign relations and a map. Lots of useful data, including lists of articles and books. The reports are inexpensive. They are bought separately, in groups or complete sets. They are updated in groups of about 60 every other year. SOURCE: Superintendent of Documents, Government Printing Office, Washington, DC 20402-9325. 1-202-647-6575.

## *Dealing with Opponent Styles, Strategies, and Tactics: Summary*

Opponents have a primary negotiating style and usually one, sometimes two, secondary styles. Negotiators must balance accommodating opponent style with their own style selection for each issue. Concurrently, negotiators must keep an issue focus. Negotiators need to develop diagnostic capabilities about opponent need orientations and likely tactics. They must be able to contest issues without attacking or demeaning opponents. They should avoid actions that lead opponents to defensiveness or other behavior that retards expeditious agreement. Negotiators continually work at staying credible. Both of motive and value. They must send exact messages and preserve appeal so that opponent receptivity stays high. This requires blending information to get the perception wanted. They also must be good listeners.

# CONCLUSION

Haste makes waste.
Benjamin Franklin

Impatience is the mother of stupidity.
Leonardo daVinci

Research, planning, and preparation are only valuable when used with skill, discipline, and patience during negotiations. Negotiators must develop enthusiasm for their positions coupled with conviction. This is vital to a negotiator's chances of success. Figure 14-4 is a checklist to ensure negotiator readiness and effectiveness before, during and after negotiations.

| Get Ready | Do It | Wrap It Up |
|---|---|---|
| ================ | ================ | ================ |
| Is it negotiable? | Maintain self-control. | Give nothing un-earned away. |
| Got enough data about your points? | Take steps and actions leading to sound resolutions and agreements. | Decide on how formal the agreement form must be. |
| Answered key questions about the other party? | Do not intimidate them or yourself. | Avoid introducing new faces at close. |
| Reviewed & tested your positions; used a devil's advocate; got a must list? | Keep track of things (i.e. concessions). | Summarize points & understandings;clarify definitions. |
| Need a team? | Avoid distractions.<br><br>Identify & work with all styles. | Is it a win-win, or close to it? |
| Have no concession pattern or other self-limiting habits? | Strive for "quid pro quo" maintenance. | Set up agreement monitoring necessary. |
| Know your authorized limits? | Use end probes (no loose ends). | Recap data about the other party for future use; share what was learned with others. |
| | Define terms. | |
| | Concentrate; listen. | |

**Figure 14-4.** CHECKLIST for before, during and after negotiations (Source: Sparks Consultants)

# APPENDIX

## Checklists

Negotiating is a complex process. Any such process is helped by using formatted methods like checklists. These ensure that the things that must be done are. The examples given are to stimulate ideas about the aids negotiators might design. They are primarily for the sale of a product or service. Other forms are needed for negotiating

- with governmental agencies,
- in collective bargaining with unions,
- for loans,
- real estate, and
- divestitures or acquisitions.

---

**For opponent:**

1. What is its industry position in
    a. market share
    b. technical competence
    c. financial strength and profitability
    d. management?
2. What is its reputation (include source)?
3. What is the record with opponent?  Past relations and performance in
    a. service
    b. quality
    c. cooperation
    d. flexibility
    e. reliability
    f. limitations?
4. What future relationship do we want with them
    a. short term
    b. long term?

**For negotiator:**

1. What are the structural considerations
    a. style we should try
    b. authority we will have
    c. timing we must meet or schedule
    d. location preferred
    e. people representing us (names, skills)?
2. What are the issues
    a. major - strengths and weaknesses
    b. minor - strengths and weaknesses?
3. What is our starting position or issue
    a. strategy
    b. tactics?

---

**Figure A-1.** Checklist for reviewing key areas prior to analyzing issues.

## Goals and objectives

1. Scope, description of work needed
2. Specification and standards
3. Schedule requirements
4. Conditions
   a. risks
   b. liabilities
   c. warranties
   d. concessions
   e. special clearances
5. Price range, internal cost analysis and projections

## Priorities

1. Facts set and separated from assumptions
2. Matrix made
3. "Must list" made
4. Secondary issues clarified
5. Agenda developed

## Strategic considerations

1. Type of contract
   a. fixed price
   b. cost plus
   c. other
2. Bargaining position
   a. urgency
   b. market conditions
   c. local constraints
3. Research on opponent
4. Estimated opponent needs, wants and options
5. Selected setting
6. Opening position desired

## Team composition

1. Establish roles
2. Explain control procedures

**Figure A-2.** Position checklist.

1. Are we compartmentalized [gives opponent advantage of working against nonunified group]?
2. Do we have a pattern [opponent can design a strategy to better us]?
3. Do we keep commercial [money] separate from technical [capability] considerations?
4. Do we assess past record of opponent [follow up]?
5. Is our expertise ample [to keep power balanced]?
6. Are we overgenerous because of size or circumstance?
7. Are we comfortable in severe conflict situations?
8. Have our must lists been satisfactory?
9. Are we patient enough with opponents who are slow to see larger aspects of an issue?
10. Are our communications concise?
11. Do we keep quid pro quo for concessions?
12. Do we avoid suboptimizing within [can opponent find which area is dominant and play to its needs]?
13. Are our agreement format and terms clear, their meaning definite?
14. Do we allow opponent enough time to present their side [do we hurry to the center of things and miss important data]?
15. Are our team members disciplined?
16. Do we establish ranges that have proved realistic?
17. Do we use recesses well, avoid impulse control and over-involvement?
18. Are we overbearing and responsible for making negotiations more difficult [like give opponents a reason to be uncooperative]?

**Figure A-3.** Checklist to identify weakness due to internal shortcomings.

1. Are there ambiguous statements and clauses?

   Examples
   What would be considered reasonable to both parties?
   Under emergency conditions, what will one party expect to get or be willing to give?

2. Are specifications precise?

   Examples
   Do both parties have the same data for the agreement?
   Have agreed to changes been recorded by both parties?

3. Are time and rate term precise?

   Examples
   Is week defined by days or hours?
   Is the number of hours per day defined?
   Is it clear what is overtime and when it starts?
   Is travel time allowance specified?
   Is travel time paid; at what rate?

4. Are terms tight or loose?

   Examples
   Are initials used where words should be written out?
   Are acknowledgements specified by time?

5. Shopping list contracts:

   Examples
   Are usages verified?
   Are general service type contracts backed by verified usage amounts?

6. Are escalation clauses specific?

   Examples
   Are terms set out for interest by amount and type [compound or simple]?
   Can delivery slippage give opponent an advantage due to escalation clause wording?
   Are penalty clauses ambiguous?

**Figure A-4.** Checklist for finding pitfalls in terms and conditions.

| ITEMS | CONTRIBUTION TO OUTCOME | | | | |
|---|---|---|---|---|---|
| | 4 | 3 | 2 | 1 | 0 |
| **Startup** | | | | | |
| 1. Environment: | | | | | |
| physical setting, amenities | | | | | |
| 2. Projected image: | | | | | |
| where authority lies. | | | | | |
| 3. Agenda: | | | | | |
| reviewed, altered. | | | | | |
| | | | | | |
| **Negotiation sessions** | | | | | |
| 1. Understanding agreement | | | | | |
| terms/conditions. | | | | | |
| 2. Opponent: | | | | | |
| performance, capabilities. | | | | | |
| 3. Communications: | | | | | |
| clear, effective. | | | | | |
| 4. Closure techniques: | | | | | |
| items tacked down. | | | | | |
| 5. Goals: | | | | | |
| Could performance have been better? | | | | | |
| Can agreement be administered | | | | | |
| Were economics in line? | | | | | |
| | | | | | |
| **Critique** | | | | | |
| 1. Was preparation adequate? | | | | | |
| 2. Was team effective? | | | | | |
| 3. Were individuals effective? | | | | | |
| | | | | | |
| **Summary** | | | | | |
| 1. Conclusions: | | | | | |
| recommendations reached; | | | | | |
| goals reached. | | | | | |
| 2. Wins: | | | | | |
| How were gains made?; | | | | | |
| where did things work out poorly? | | | | | |
| TOTALS ⟶ | | | | | |
| 4 = Excellent to 1 = poor | | | | | |
| 0 = Not applicable | | | | | |

**Figure A-5.** Evaluating negotiations.

Contractor/vendor_____File #_____

Address_____Date_____

Scope of work/job title

Duration of agreement_____yr[s]_____mo[s]_____wk[s]

Agreement #_____Value $_____

Rating ( ✓ one box only) • pre   • post   • combined

| Description | Good | Okay | Poor | Not rated |
|---|---|---|---|---|
| 1. Labor adequacy | 0 | 0 | 0 | 0 |
| 2. Supervision qualification | 0 | 0 | 0 | 0 |
| 3. (a) Safety compliance | 0 | 0 | 0 | 0 |
| (b) Understood job & performance requirements. | 0 | 0 | 0 | 0 |
| 4. Schedule adherence | 0 | 0 | 0 | 0 |
| 5. Cooperation | 0 | 0 | 0 | 0 |
| 6. Overall performance | 0 | 0 | 0 | 0 |
| 7. Other (describe) | 0 | 0 | 0 | 0 |
| 8. | 0 | 0 | 0 | 0 |
| 9. | 0 | 0 | 0 | 0 |

Additional work

Disputes (attach full description)

Remarks

Discussed with contractor/vendor • yes     Date_____ • no
Contractor comments

Originator's signature

**Figure A-6.** Evaluating contractor/vendor performance.

Description_____Reference#_____
Our estimate pre-negotiation    $_____Date_____
Bid accepted                    $_____
Negotiated value                $_____

Our team names                  Titles              Departments




Opponents                       Titles              Styles



_____

Comments

                                Rank                Disposition
Issue(s)                        Major Minor         Resolved  Stalemate
Ours




Opponents




Duration of Negotiation_____

Recommended future improvements: specific points that will improve our near term performance.




Signature/Title_____

**Figure A-7.** Evaluation/critique: negotiation performance.

# Bibliography

There are many books that tell the use of negotiating techniques. The books listed give a deeper understanding of what happens when these techniques are used.

Berne, Eric, Games People Play. N. Y.: Grove Press, 1964.

Chapman, A. H., Put Offs & Come Ons. N. Y.: G. P Putnam's Sons, 1968.

Cooper, Gary L. (ed.), Theories of Group Process. N. Y.: John Wiley and Sons,1975.

Collins, Larry, and Lapierre Dominique, Freedom at Midnight. N. Y.: Simon & Schuster, 1975.

David M. Kennedy Center for International Studies, Culturgrams. Golden: Brigham Young University, Annual.

Delbecq, A. L., A. H. Van de Ven and D. H. Gustafson, Group Techniques for Program Planning. Glenview: Scott Foresman & Co., 1975.

Franklin, Benjamin, Poor Richard's Almanacs (1733-1758). N. Y.: George Macy Companies, 1964.

Hoviand, J. K., Psychology of Communication and Persuasion. New Haven: Yale Press.

Jepson, R. W., Clear Thinking. London: Longmans, Green & Co 1955.

Jay, Anthony, Management And Machiavelli. N. Y.: Holt, Rinehart and Winston, 1967.

Ibid. The New Oratory. N. Y: American Management Association, 1971.

Lee, Irving, How to Talk with People. N. Y.: Harper, 1952.

Luscher, Max, The Four Color Person. N. Y.: Simon & Shuster, 1979.

Mehrabian, Albert, Silent Messages. Belmont: Wadsworth Publishing Co., 1971.

Rapoport, Anatol, Flights, Games and Debates. Ann Arbor: The University of Michigan, 1966.

Schoenbum, David, Triumph In Paris. N. Y.: Harper & Row, 1976.

Stabbing, L. S., Thinking to Some Purpose. N. Y.: Penguin Books, 1959.

Schwartz, Tony, The Responsive Chord. Garden City: Anchor Books, 1973.

U.S. Department of State, Background Notes. Washington: Superintendent of Documents, Government Printing Office, Annual.

Williams, Frederick, Reasoning With Statistics. N.Y.: Holt, Rinehart & Winston, 1978.

# Index